MW01156933

The Whelping and Rearing of Puppies
A Complete and Practical Guide

by Muriel P. Lee

TS-288

Dedication

To all the little mothers and their midwives.

Title Page: Litter of Samoyed pups at six weeks of age — almost ready for new homes. Breeders, Jim and Elfie Shea.

Photography: Thanks to the many breeders and photographers who supplied photographs.

Illustrated by: E. Joanne Cummins. Hand writing in whelping notes by Janice Malueg.

© by T.F.H. Publications, Inc.

Distributed in the UNITED STATES to the Pet Trade by T.F.H. Publications, Inc., One T.F.H. Plaza, Neptune City, NJ 07753; distributed in the UNITED STATES to the Bookstore and Library Trade by National Book Network, Inc. 4720 Boston Way, Lanham MD 20706; in CANADA to the Pet Trade by H & L Pet Supplies Inc., 27 Kingston Crescent, Kitchener, Ontario N2B 2T6; Rolf C. Hagen Inc., 3225 Sartelon St. Laurent-Montreal Quebec H4R 1E8; in CANADA to the Book Trade by Vanwell Publishing Ltd., 1 Northrup Crescent, St. Catharines, Ontario L2M 6P5 ; in ENGLAND by T.F.H. Publications, PO Box 15, Waterlooville PO7 6BQ; in AUSTRALIA AND THE SOUTH PACIFIC by T.F.H. (Australia), Pty. Ltd., Box 149, Brookvale 2100 N.S.W., Australia; in NEW ZEALAND by Brooklands Aquarium Ltd. 5 McGiven Drive, New Plymouth, RD1 New Zealand; in Japan by T.F.H. Publications, Japan—Jiro Tsuda, 10-12-3 Ohjidai, Sakura, Chiba 285, Japan; in SOUTH AFRICA by Lopis (Pty) Ltd., P.O. Box 39127, Booysens, 2016, Johannesburg, South Africa. Published by T.F.H. Publications, Inc.
MANUFACTURED IN THE
UNITED STATES OF AMERICA
BY T.F.H. PUBLICATIONS, INC.

The Whelping and Rearing of Puppies
A Complete and Practical Guide

by Muriel P. Lee

Contents

Introduction....6

About the Author....7

Your Bitch Has Been Bred.....8
The Whelping Box

Whelping Equipment.....13

The Whelping Is Expected Soon.....17
Some General Concerns before Whelping Time • The Temperature Has Dropped

Labor Begins: Whelping Follows.....23
Assisting as each Whelp is Born • Onward with the Whelping • When the Whelping is Finished • Whelping Box Environment • Weather: How the Heat and Cold Affect a Litter • Supplements

Whelping Problems.....37
Labor Starts and a Whelp Does Not Appear • A Large Whelp • Presentation of the Waterbag Only • Appearance of the Head Only • Digital Examination of the Bitch • Presentation of the Whelp in the Birth Canal • Malpresentation • Uterine Inertia • Summary

When to Have a Cesarean Section.....45
Emergency Veterinary Service • A Note on Traveling to the Veterinarian • What is a Cesarean Section? • Accepting the Pups after a Cesarean Section • Getting the Mother and the Pups Settled In

Newborn Pups.....58
Slow Starting Pups • What To Do with a Slow Starting Pup • How to Tell the Boys from the Girls • Good Mothers (Or Super Moms) • Defective Pups

The First Five Days.....67

Keep the Whelping Box Clean • Care for the Mother • Care for the Pups • Healthy Pups and Sickly Pups • What Causes Sickly Pups? • The Joy of a Healthy Pup

Treating Sickly Pups.....73

Handling the Sickly Pup • Death is Coming

Possible Problems for a Nursing Bitch.....77

Caked Breasts (Galactostasis) • Mastitis • Toxic Milk • Eclampsia (Milk Fever) • Failure to Accept Pups • How to Separate the Bitch from Her Pups-Orphan Puppies

Raising Pups by Hand.....84

Keeping the Pups Warm • Nourishment • Bottle Feeding • Tube Feeding • Cleaning the Orphan Pup • Important Tips

Your Puppies Are Growing.....94

Weaning • Care for the Mother • Food Pans • Water • General Information • Daily Puppy Care

Puppies from Four to Eight Weeks.....100

Socializing: Some Common—And Not So Common—Puppy Problems • Puppy Shots • Parvovirus • Puppy Bites • Injuries • Swimmers • Prolasped Rectum • Umbilical Hernias-Coccidiosis

Wrapping Up the Litter.....112

Registration Forms, Contracts and Breeding Records • Selling Your Pups

Some Conclusions......121

Index.....124

Introduction

I originally wrote and published the *Whelping and Rearing of Puppies* in 1984 as I felt that a single source of information in a how-to manual was needed to assist breeders with their whelping and puppy rearing. It has been gratifying through the years, and through numerous printings, to see that the book has continued to do well. I am very pleased that TFH Publications, Inc. has taken over the publishing of the book, as the advice within will now be supplemented by many color pictures.

The manual is a guide for whelping puppies that is tempered with common sense. Your family, job and social life continue on with or without a litter. You are working with nature, and some pups will live and some will die. You will be given hints and instructions about how to minimize problems, how to work with your veterinarian and how to enjoy the litter to the fullest without disrupting your lifestyle for two, or more, months.

Before starting this book, I wrote to 27 breeders requesting information about their whelping equipment, their whelping problems and their puppy care. These breeders, taken together, have produced a total of 1043 litters over a period of 449 years and have whelped approximately 5000 puppies! Without a doubt, experience speaks through the survey. After each section of the book I have noted what actions the breeders take and do not take in specific situations and what they do or do not look for. Interesting comments from them are also presented. Most of these breeders have produced Best in Show dogs, specialty winners, top producers and group winners. These breeders not only have been around the whelping box a long time, but they have been in the show ring, and they look at the world of dogs with a practical eye.

To the novice, this "eye" may occasionally appear hard or uncaring. But if your want to be a successful breeder (and a successful breeder is one who produces winners) over the long haul — 20 or 30 years —your whelping and puppy rearing must be seasoned with sound thinking and practicality.

To all of you, may you have many future winners in your whelping boxes and may this book help you to whelp the winners of the future!

Muriel P. Lee

About the Author

Muriel Lee has been active in the dog world since 1965 when she purchased her first Old English Sheepdog. After finishing four Old English champions, she decided to find a breed that was less bulky and easier to keep. Having grown up with a Wire Fox terrier, she found it natural to look at the terrier group and eventually settled upon a Scottish Terrier. Over the years she has shown many a Scot and whelped numerous litters for both herself and for her close friend, John Sheehan of Firebrand Kennels.

In 1984 she wrote and published her first book, *The Whelping and Rearing of Puppies: A Complete and Practical Guide.* In 1993 TFH Publications brought out her book, *The Official Book of the Scottish Terrier* and she is currently under contract for several other breed-specific books.

She has been a member of the Minneapolis Kennel Club for 30 years, serving as treasurer for 20 years. She is a member of the Lake Minnetonka Kennel Club and a member of the Scottish Terrier Club of America where she has been historian and editor of the Scottish Terrier Club of America's yearbooks. She is an AKC licensed judge of Scottish Terriers and has frequently given lectures on the whelping of puppies.

Muriel was a self-employed businesswoman in Minneapolis for 22 years, owning a drinking and eating establishment just off the University of Minnesota campus. She is a graduate of the University of Minnesota with a degree in music, an avid gardener, and is proficient in needlework, having had her pieces exhibited in Minneapolis, Charleston, Dallas and Monaco, in addition to the American Kennel Club "Bitches in Stitches" exhibition in 1982.

Muriel resides in a townhouse with a nine-year-old "Morris" cat, a six-year-old French Bulldog, Ch. Bushaway Remy LeFox and a young Frenchie pup, Bushaway Bijou LeFox.

Your Bitch Has Been Bred

Let's start with the assumption that you have put some thought into the breeding of your bitch, that you have found the best mate available for her and that the breeding has taken place. Is she pregnant? If you are eager to

thirtieth day, fluids start building up in her system, making it more difficult to feel the walnut-sized (or smaller) whelps. This is not a foolproof system, as bitches, especially of the heavier bodied breeds, can carry their pups high,

The noticeably larger stomach and enlarged nipples of this Viszla are clear indications of pregnancy.

know and you do not want to wait the four or five weeks it takes until she begins to look pregnant, take her to your veterinarian on or about the twenty-sixth day following the breeding date. Through palpation he can often tell if she is pregnant. After the

and it can be difficult to feel them. If your bitch is carrying only one or two pups, it can be harder yet to detect them.

By the fifth week—and certainly by the sixth—your girl should be spreading out a bit on the sides, and her stomach will be noticeably larger. (Sometimes the bitch suddenly expands overnight, and then you *know* that she is pregnant.) She may be quieter and may act more lovingly toward all of the family members. Often, as early as three weeks, her nipples will start to enlarge and turn a pinkish color—a good sign but not always a reliable one. (A sad day, sixty-four days after breeding: "Oh! Pink boobies and no babies!")

By the sixth and seventh weeks she should be looking and acting pregnant. You can compare the nine-week gestation period to that of a woman's pregnancy—one week to each month. You should now be following some simple guidelines.

1) Do not overfeed your bitch. It's easy to do because she seems to be hungry all the time, but extra weight can make the delivery more difficult.

2) Exercise your bitch daily. Take her out for a walk once a day. As her whelping approaches, shorten the distance of the walk.

3) Feed properly. Supplements are unnecessary if you are feeding a nationally known dog food. Dog food manufacturers spend millions of dollars a year on scientists, veterinarians and feeding programs in order to come up with the most nutritious formulas. After the fifth week or so of the pregnancy, you may want to divide the bitch's meal and feed her half in the A.M. and half in the P.M. During the end of pregnancy, it will be difficult for her to eat a full meal at one sitting.

4) Do not worm your bitch or give her antibiotics during the gestation period unless your veterinarian recommends the treatment. You should have wormed your bitch before breeding her. If you did not and you suspect that she is wormy, wait until the puppies are weaned and then worm her *and* the pups after getting a stool analysis.

5) Provide extra care in the last week of pregnancy. If your bitch is one of the short-legged breeds, you may have to carry her up and down stairs during the last week or so of the pregnancy. Whether she is long-legged or short-legged, try to keep her from jumping on and off the furniture, bed or porch. During the last four or five days of pregnancy, you can often feel the whelps moving about. If your bitch lies on your lap, it is easy to feel movement; also, by placing your hands alongside the loins and applying a little pressure, you usually can feel them move.

During the last week your bitch may have some "accidents" in the house. Pressure builds up against the bladder, and she is not always able to keep from urinating. Let her outside more frequently to relieve herself. Also, in the last week of pregnancy, the backbone of your bitch will become very prominent. As the stomach becomes distended with the whelps, the backbone becomes more gaunt or "roachy." At this point your bitch may not look like the show girl she was a few months previously, but don't despair—her beauty will return.

THE WHELPING BOX

If this is your first litter and you are certain your bitch is pregnant, start giving some thought to the whelping box. (Do wait until you are sure that puppies are on the way, since an unused whelping box presents great storage problems. A used box also presents storage problems, but at least you get your money's worth out of the box.) If you plan to have only one or two litters in your lifetime, you may want to either borrow a box from someone or else build one. The box should be large enough to allow one to one-and-a-half feet of space around the bitch when she is lying in it on her side. It is not necessary to have a huge box for mother and pups to wander around in. The majority of breeders surveyed used wooden whelping boxes, and one-fourth of them used a commercial whelping pen. The box should stand at least two

A wooden whelping box of a more complicated design.

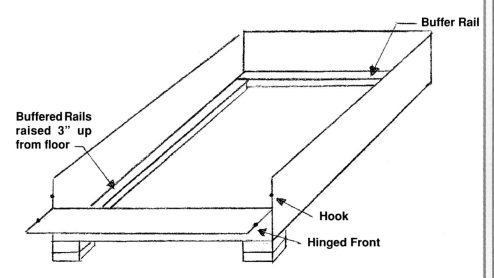

Buffer Rail

Buffered Rails raised 3" up from floor

Hook

Hinged Front

Floor or Base, 1 piece of plywood the desired size
3 - 1 x 12" for sides, cut to proper lengths
2 - 1 x 6" for hinged front, cut to proper lengths
Four 1/2 x 3" Buffer Rails, cut to proper lengths
2 Hinges
2 Hooks
* Nails or Wood Screws
L Braces to attach Buffer Rails
Pieces of 2 x 4's for legs
Vinyl to cover bottom of box
Spar varnish if desired

* Wood screws prefered over nails

1) Can disassemble in box and store easily.
2) No chance of puppy getting speared by a nail point protruding from wood into interior of box.

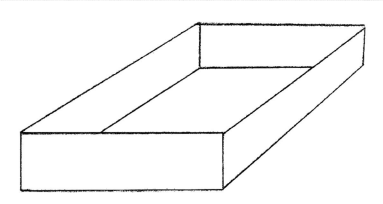

1" Floor or base - piece of plywood cut to desired size
Four 1 x 12's cut to proper size
Wooden screws or nails
Vinyl to cover bottom of box

This is a box to be used once or twice and disposed of.
Note: 1) There are no buffer rails.
2) Front lid is not hinged so you may have to lift mother in and out.
3) No legs so box rests directly on floor.
4) No varnish so box will not be as clean or as sanitary as box A.

A wooden whelping box of a simple design.

inches off the floor to keep it free from drafts. Using screws to put the box together will allow you to take it apart, to stack the pieces together, and to store it easily. If your box is not too large, it can be hung on the garage wall when not in use.

If you have a small to medium-sized breed and you are planning to have four or five litters over a several-year span, you may wish to invest in a whelping pen. The advantages to this type of pen are that it is collapsible and easily stored and can be washed and sanitized between litters. In addition, you can purchase legs and raise the pen to a comfortable height so that you avoid the strain of constant bending.

Several breeders use children's swimming pools. Others use a cardboard box. If you are expecting more than one litter, you can become quite creative for the second whelping pen. Whatever you use, remember that it is essential to keep drafts off your puppies and to keep the pen or box clean.

If you have a small to medium-sized breed, like the Scottish Terrier, and plan to have a number of litters over several years, you might want to invest in a collapsible whelping pen that can be sanitized, stored and then re-used when needed.

BREEDERS' SURVEY

What is the construction of your whelping box?

Wooden <u>18</u>   Whelping pen <u>7</u>

Crates <u>3</u>   Cardboard Boxes <u>2</u>

Does the box or pen sit on the floor or is it elevated?

Seventeen of the breeders raised their boxes, and eleven left them on the floor. The heights of the raised boxes varied from two to twenty-four inches.

Some breeders prefer to use a cardboard box lined with plastic and newspaper as a whelping pen. This Australian Terrier dam watches over her two-week-old pups.

Whelping Equipment

Set up your whelping pen or box about ten days before you anticipate the whelping, and put your bitch in it several times a day. Although she will stay in it only for a few minutes at a time, she will learn that this space belongs to her. She may urinate in the box the first few times you put her in it. She is urinating more at this point because her stomach is full of puppies, and she is also marking off her territory. Place your box in a quiet part of the house. A spare bedroom that is not being used is ideal. I like to use the dining room so that I can hear the puppies from the kitchen. They are out of the way there, yet I have easy access to the dam for feeding and exercising. Wherever you put your box, keep it out of drafts and keep it in a fairly quiet area. Some breeders like to keep their puppies in their bedroom for the first week, but this is not really necessary. It is bound to disrupt your sleep at a time when you need a good night's rest in order to cope with the extra work and care.

Decide what kind of bedding to put in your whelping box. Most of the breeders surveyed used newspapers and/or towels for bedding. I prefer to use old bath towels. (Family members are usually happy to pass along old towels.) Some of my bitches have shredded newspapers so vigorously that paper has gotten stuck between their teeth and this has formed a papermache wad inside the mouth. When this happens, the jaws become stuck together and another person is needed to hold the bitch's head while you pry the paper out of the mouth. I

Place your whelping pen in a quiet area away from drafts, where you can hear the puppies and have easy access to the mother if necessary.

have heard of this happening to other breeders, but none of the breeders surveyed reported having had this problem. Whatever you use for bedding, you will probably have to change it several times during the whelping, depending on the size of the litter.

You should have the following items on hand for the actual whelping:
1) Whelping box
2) Many towels
3) Scissors (cleaned with alcohol)
4) Paper and pencil
5) Watch or clock
6) A "ready" box with several towels in it
7) Hot water bottle
8) Paper towels
9) Newspapers
10) Phone number of your veterinarian and an emergency veterinary night service
11) Several large plastic bags

Some optional items that you may want:
1) Reflector shade with a light bulb and, if necessary, an extension cord
2) Scale (a food scale will do)
3) Artery forceps

Let's look at each of these items separately so that you will understand their function.

Whelping Box. The box should be sitting in a quiet corner, clean and ready to go.

Towels. You may want to use towels instead of newspapers to line the bottom of your whelping box. You need towels to rub your puppies dry. And you also need towels for the ready box. If you do a lot of hand wringing, it's nice to have a few towels handy.

Scissors. You may have to cut one or more umbilical cords, so you will need scissors that have been cleaned in alcohol.

Paper and Pencil. It is very important to mark down the time that your bitch goes into labor and to note whether it is hard labor. Record the time that all of the whelping activities occur. This record is important for two reasons: a significant lapse of time between puppies—or between the onset of labor and the first delivery—tells you that you are having a problem. If you have to call the veterinarian, he will need to know the amount of time that has passed between each activity.

Ready Box. The ready box can be a cardboard or a gift box. Put several towels in the bottom of it. After your first pup is delivered, fill the hot water bottle, wrap it in a towel, and place it in the box. The ready box holds the pups while the bitch is delivering the next puppy. You will find many additional uses for this box as the days go by. A beer carton can work very well.

Hot Water Bottle. See above.

Newspapers. If you are using newspapers during the whelping, you should change them periodically. If you are using only towels, you should line your box with papers after the whelping is completed.

Veterinarian's Phone Number. In case you need to call for help, have the veterinarian's number near at hand.

Plastic Bags. Large plastic garbage bags are useful for holding dirty towels or newspapers. There is a certain aroma surrounding whelping. Tucking away dirty towels and papers as you go along will help to dissipate the "whelping" smell.

Reflector Shade. A reflector shade is really essential in cold weather. Put in a forty or sixty watt bulb and clamp the shade on the side of the pen or the back of a chair. Aim it at about half of the pen or box. The lamp will provide the pups with extra warmth and heat, and mother can move to the darker side of the pen if she gets too warm. A word about the various kinds of heating units that can be used for whelping puppies. Many breeders surveyed used both infra-red bulbs and heating pads, but either can dehydrate a puppy. Hot water bottles and reflector shades with a regular bulb will give the needed warmth without dehydrating the pups.

Scale. Many breeders weigh their pups at birth, and many continue to weigh them daily for the first week—and then weekly thereafter. Weighing is not essential, but the information can be useful. If you have to raise a pup or litter by hand, you have to have a scale, since the amount of feeding formula is determined by the pup's weight. Any scale that measures in ounces will work well.

Artery Forceps. Artery forceps can be used for pulling out a retained afterbirth, provided that you have an end of a cord to grasp. If a pup's umbilical cord persists in bleeding, you can clamp the forceps on it for a few minutes.

BREEDERS' SURVEY

Most of the breeders preferred a spare bedroom for their whelping. Dens, basements, kennel rooms and utility rooms are also popular. Rooms that are warm, quiet and unused during the whelping period are most often used.

Of the twenty-seven breeders surveyed, twenty used newspapers for bedding in the whelping box, and seven did not use newspapers at all. Some used a combination of newspapers and towels. Four used old blankets. One liked pillow cases, and others preferred mattress pads and rugs. Newspapers and towels are the most popular bedding materials, but there are other options as well. Keep in mind that you must use either disposable materials (newspapers) or materials that can be easily washed and dried. Most breeders agreed that a litter of puppies results in an endless stream of washing.

Extras. It is always nice to have a coffee pot on; the entire whelping process will probably take at least three hours—and it can go on for six or eight hours or more. Reading material helps to pass the time while you wait for action to begin or to continue. I do a lot of knitting or needlework during whelping time. Simply sitting, waiting, and watching can become tedious!

You are now ready for the action, and, with some luck, it will take place in the morning or afternoon rather than in the wee hours of the A.M.—or during a holiday weekend. A word of warning: many litters seem to come in the early morning hours, during the weekends, or in the middle of a nice dinner party. I've sat through a Cesarean on a Christmas afternoon and delivered puppies on New Year's Eve. I've had a litter whelped at midnight when I have had to get up at 6:00 a.m. for a dog show. You get no choice.

Examples of some of the whelping equipment you will need to have on hand include: towels, a scale, a "ready" box, newspapers, a reflector shade with an extension cord, a clock, plastic bags, scissors, forceps and paper and pencil.

The Whelping Is Expected Soon

The Perpetual Whelping Calendar can tell you when to expect the whelping. To use it, check the date that your bitch was bred and then check the next column over to see when she is due to whelp. The gestation period for dogs is sixty-three days, and your pups can come anytime after the fifty-eighth day. Arrival before the fifty-eighth day is a sign that something is wrong; however, this is an unusual occurrence. If your bitch was bred two times—on June 1st and June 3rd for instance—you can expect puppies anytime between July 29th (fifty-eight days after the first breeding) and August 5th (sixty-three days after the second breeding). If there was an additional breeding on June 5th, the due date would extend to August 7th. The best way to figure it is that the puppies will come around August 2nd or 3rd, the midpoint between all of these breedings.

The week before the whelping you can take your bitch to the veterinarian for an x-ray. This can be helpful, but if the x-ray is not read accurately you can be misled about the number of pups to expect. Breeders in the survey rarely used this device, and they used it only when they thought that there might be problems.

Do not be concerned about your pups coming early: they rarely appear before the sixty-first day following the first breeding, and it is not unusual for them to go to the sixty-third day following the last breeding. Do not let your bitch go beyond the sixty-third day without contacting your veterinarian. If she should go beyond the last due date, call the veterinarian and follow his advice. He may have you come in with your bitch, or he may tell you to wait another day or two, especially if she is showing no indication of the onset of labor and no signs of distress.

You now know within a week or so just when to expect the puppies. You can pinpoint the time by monitoring your bitch's temperature. Use a rectal thermometer and dip the end of it in petroleum jelly to facilitate insertion. A dog's normal temperature fluctuates between 101 and 102 degrees. Twenty-four to forty-eight hours before whelping, the temperature will drop to 99 degrees or 98 degrees—or even 96 degrees. It is not unusual for the temperature to drop to 99 degrees and then within an hour or so to move back to 101 degrees. When the temperature drops and stays depressed, the

Spring is a great time to plan for the arrival of a litter because of the warmer weather and the ample opportunities for socialization. This Golden Retriever pup is owned by Barbara McKee.

PERPETUAL WHELPING CHART

Bred / Due	Days →																														
Bred—Jan.	1	2	3	4	5	6	7	8	9	10	11	12	13	14	15	16	17	18	19	20	21	22	23	24	25	26	27	28	29	30	31
Due—March	5	6	7	8	9	10	11	12	13	14	15	16	17	18	19	20	21	22	23	24	25	26	27	28	29	30	31	*April* 1	2	3	4
Bred—Feb.	1	2	3	4	5	6	7	8	9	10	11	12	13	14	15	16	17	18	19	20	21	22	23	24	25	26	27	28			
Due—April	5	6	7	8	9	10	11	12	13	14	15	16	17	18	19	20	21	22	23	24	25	26	27	28	29	30	*May* 1	2			
Bred—Mar.	1	2	3	4	5	6	7	8	9	10	11	12	13	14	15	16	17	18	19	20	21	22	23	24	25	26	27	28	29	30	31
Due—May	3	4	5	6	7	8	9	10	11	12	13	14	15	16	17	18	19	20	21	22	23	24	25	26	27	28	29	30	31	*June* 1	2
Bred—Apr.	1	2	3	4	5	6	7	8	9	10	11	12	13	14	15	16	17	18	19	20	21	22	23	24	25	26	27	28	29	30	
Due—June	3	4	5	6	7	8	9	10	11	12	13	14	15	16	17	18	19	20	21	22	23	24	25	26	27	28	29	30	*July* 1	2	
Bred—May	1	2	3	4	5	6	7	8	9	10	11	12	13	14	15	16	17	18	19	20	21	22	23	24	25	26	27	28	29	30	31
Due—July	3	4	5	6	7	8	9	10	11	12	13	14	15	16	17	18	19	20	21	22	23	24	25	26	27	28	29	30	31	*August* 1	2
Bred—June	1	2	3	4	5	6	7	8	9	10	11	12	13	14	15	16	17	18	19	20	21	22	23	24	25	26	27	28	29	30	
Due—August	3	4	5	6	7	8	9	10	11	12	13	14	15	16	17	18	19	20	21	22	23	24	25	26	27	28	29	30	31	*Sept.* 1	
Bred—July	1	2	3	4	5	6	7	8	9	10	11	12	13	14	15	16	17	18	19	20	21	22	23	24	25	26	27	28	29	30	31
Due—September	2	3	4	5	6	7	8	9	10	11	12	13	14	15	16	17	18	19	20	21	22	23	24	25	26	27	28	29	30	*Oct.* 1	2
Bred—Aug.	1	2	3	4	5	6	7	8	9	10	11	12	13	14	15	16	17	18	19	20	21	22	23	24	25	26	27	28	29	30	31
Due—October	3	4	5	6	7	8	9	10	11	12	13	14	15	16	17	18	19	20	21	22	23	24	25	26	27	28	29	30	31	*Nov.* 1	2
Bred—Sept.	1	2	3	4	5	6	7	8	9	10	11	12	13	14	15	16	17	18	19	20	21	22	23	24	25	26	27	28	29	30	
Due—November	3	4	5	6	7	8	9	10	11	12	13	14	15	16	17	18	19	20	21	22	23	24	25	26	27	28	29	30	*Dec.* 1	2	
Bred—Oct.	1	2	3	4	5	6	7	8	9	10	11	12	13	14	15	16	17	18	19	20	21	22	23	24	25	26	27	28	29	30	31
Due—December	3	4	5	6	7	8	9	10	11	12	13	14	15	16	17	18	19	20	21	22	23	24	25	26	27	28	29	30	31	*Jan.* 1	2
Bred—Nov.	1	2	3	4	5	6	7	8	9	10	11	12	13	14	15	16	17	18	19	20	21	22	23	24	25	26	27	28	29	30	
Due—January	3	4	5	6	7	8	9	10	11	12	13	14	15	16	17	18	19	20	21	22	23	24	25	26	27	28	29	30	31	*Feb.* 1	
Bred—Dec.	1	2	3	4	5	6	7	8	9	10	11	12	13	14	15	16	17	18	19	20	21	22	23	24	25	26	27	28	29	30	31
Due—February	2	3	4	5	6	7	8	9	10	11	12	13	14	15	16	17	18	19	20	21	22	23	24	25	26	27	28	*March* 1	2	3	4

whelping is due. I start taking the temperature on the fifty-eighth day from the first breeding. I take it once in the morning for several days, which tells me the bitch's normal temperature. When I think that the whelping date is closing in, I take it two or three times a day. I have to admit that if I have something interesting planned I take her temperature often. Big brunch in the A.M.? If the temperature is 101 degrees at midnight, you can probably plan on attending!

moving back in her body—to the rear—getting ready for delivery. The vulva begins to distend, and the whole area becomes soft. By putting your hands against the loins, you can often feel puppies moving. By putting your hands against the stomach, you also can tell how far the stomach is distended—and perhaps, how uncomfortable she must be.

Now it is time to do a little trimming and grooming on the mother. Clip the hair around the vulva and the mammary glands.

BREEDERS' SURVEY

Do you x-ray your bitches before whelping?
Yes 5   No 22

Those who checked "yes" said that they only x-ray "sometime." All found x-rays to be helpful, and four of the five found them to be accurate.

Remember, you only have to insert the thermometer for a minute or so. While you are taking the temperature, check the vulva of your bitch. As she nears the whelping date, she produces a clear, sticky discharge, an indication that the passage is being lubricated for the delivery of the whelps. It is not unusual for her to emit a rather "fishy" odor around the rear during this period. Even though you wash her down, the odor will return quickly.

Notice that the shape of your bitch begins to change as she nears "D Day." The pups are

If your breed is heavy or long-coated, you may want to cut the skirts back. It is not necessary to clip the hair on the stomach area down to the skin, but do cut the hair around the nipples, especially if you have a long-coated breed. If you wish to show your bitch in a few months, keep the clipping to a bare minimum. No matter how you clip, a certain amount of coat is going to be lost. Wash her stomach and rear, sponging particularly well around the nipples. If the breed is a short-coated one, you will probably want to give a complete bath. If the breed is long-coated and you do not want to bathe fully, sponge off the coat with a germicidal soap such as green soap. Whatever you do, be sure to rinse out all of the soap. Keep taking the temperature. The time is drawing nearer....

SOME GENERAL CONCERNS BEFORE WHELPING TIME

1) **Discharges.** If you see a strangely-colored discharge coming from the vulva (brown, green, or dark red, for instance) anytime before the whelping,

the system. Occasionally they are passed as mummified puppies at the time of whelping, and sometimes they are whelped and appear as "jelly babies." For whatever reason, these puppies did not completely form and were not meant to be.

THE TEMPERATURE HAS DROPPED

Your girl has a soft vulva area; she lies quietly; and she occasionally scratches around to make a bed. She may or may not refuse food or water for up to

BREEDERS' SURVEY

Have you had any litters that have gone beyond the sixty-third day following the last breeding? Yes ___9___ No ___19___

How long did you wait before contacting your veterinarian? **Answers ranged from immediately to three days. Most called by the second day.**

take your bitch to the veterinarian immediately. Something could be wrong. Such a condition is not a common occurrence, but you should be alert to the possibility that it can happen.

2) **Labor.** If your bitch shows no signs of coming into labor by the 64th day, call your veterinarian and ask if you should be concerned.

3) **Absorption of whelps.** Bitches seldom abort puppies, but they can absorb them. In early pregnancies, these whelps are totally absorbed back into

twenty-four hours before she delivers. Don't worry about her refusal to eat.

Around this time you should put your bitch in the whelping pen. If you are using a box, your girl may jump in and out a lot trying to settle down. When she is ready to deliver, *keep her in the box. Do not let her run around the house and nest all over.* Not only will your bitch be confused by all of the running around but her activity can be very hard on your house. It is not unusual for a bitch in labor to get on a sofa and rip the seat or back apart. It is easier on you, the mother, and the house to keep the bitch confined. The advantage of a whelping *pen* is that it allows you to keep her confined until you choose to lift her out.

Once the temperature has dropped, most breeders stay close to home, making only short trips out and hurrying back to make sure that everything is all right. Labor does not begin as soon as the temperature drops; it may not begin for up to thirty-six hours.

part of the house. If you wish to have a child observe the whelping, have him or her sit quietly nearby. If he or she is old enough to understand what is going on—and knows what you expect—you can have a good assistant.

Prior to the onset of labor, your bitch will by lying stretched out in her box. She may look to you for reassurance and then look at her rear with some surprise, alarm or bewilderment. She will now start to push her rear against the wall of the whelping box. She may

BREEDERS' SURVEY

Do you sit with your bitch once she goes into labor?
Yes 27　　　No 0

(This was the only question in which the breeders were in unanimous agreement!)

When labor is imminent, your bitch will be restless and may feel a little shaky when you hold her.

Whelping is usually best accomplished on a one to one basis—that is, you and the mother. If you have a friend who is an experienced whelper, you may want him or her to assist. Another family member often serves as a good helper. Whelping is a time of stress for your bitch, so keep other dogs away from the area. Keep unnecessary people away and keep noisy children in another

occasionally tear at the towels and papers—and let out a yelp or two. At these signs, start watching for the first contractions of labor.

Stay close by your bitch once labor actually begins. Many bitches do not want their owners "hovering," but they like to know that they are in the same room. Do not sit and cuddle or baby her at this time. Let her sit quietly by herself and give her an occasional word of encouragement. Do not distract her; this is the time you want her to "get to work."

Labor Begins: Whelping Follows

There has been a lot of activity in the whelping box. Your bitch has been up and down, scratching at her bedding, giving a few yelps and looking around anxiously. Suddenly all activity ceases, and she appears to be gathering up her forces.

Labor begins when the pressure from within forces the puppies toward the pelvis. The pups have developed in the two horns of the uterus, and they start to "line up" for delivery during labor. Within twenty minutes to two hours after the first contraction, the first waterbag will appear, preceding the first whelp. The waterbag is dark in color and it has a soft texture like a plastic bag full of water. It looks like a *bubble,* and it is filled with amniotic fluid, which acts as a lubricant during whelping. Many times you will not detect the waterbag; it often breaks as it begins to protrude. Don't be alarmed if at first mother is unable to immediately push the water bag completely out. Another contraction or two may be required to break it. When the bag does break, the cervix will dilate as it prepares for the delivery of the first whelp.

Whelps should deliver at intervals ranging from fifteen minutes to three hours. Intervals of thirty to forty-five minutes seems to be most common. For example, a puppy will drop from the left

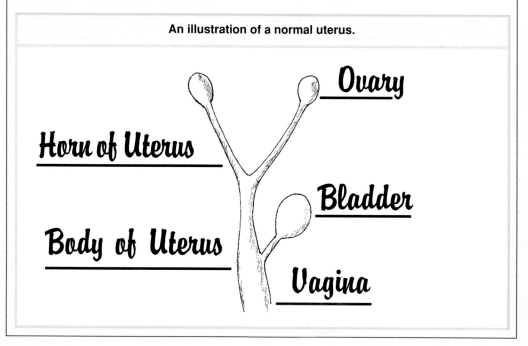

An illustration of a normal uterus.

Ovary

Horn of Uterus

Bladder

Body of Uterus

Vagina

horn, and then twenty minutes later a puppy will drop from the right horn.

Then, there may be a forty-five minute wait while more whelps "line up" for delivery. The pup closest to the vaginal opening will come out first.

During labor you can best help your bitch by sitting back and observing—and perhaps giving a few words of encouragement. Unless you have reason to believe that there will be complications, assume that all will go smoothly and that the dam will be able to do the work herself. Don't be impatient, as it may take several "heaves" before she pushes a pup out completely. If everything goes according to the "book" the whelp will come out in a rush; and the mother will reach around, tear and remove the sac, and cut the cord. During the cord cutting process, she will "bang" the pup around a bit. Do not worry, as this action stimulates the pup and helps to get it going. Once the sac is broken, she will then lick the pup vigorously. Note the time of this event on your whelping chart together with the sex of the whelp, the color, and any identifying marks. Be sure to note whether or not the afterbirth came out. Mark down anything else on this chart that you think may be of interest at a later date.

Several years ago a friend with a large working breed whelped her first litter assisted by her husband and her next door neighbor. Both women were RNs, and the breeder had worked up an elaborate whelping chart, which the husband was to supervise. The bitch whelped sixteen puppies in

An illustration of a uterus containing whelps.

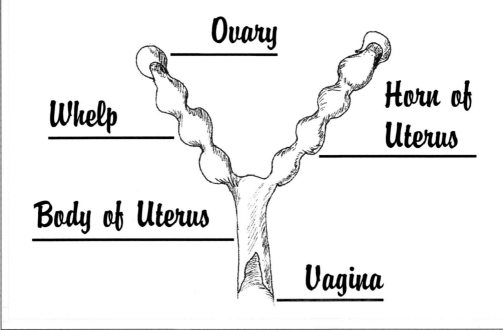

Ovary

Whelp

Horn of Uterus

Body of Uterus

Vagina

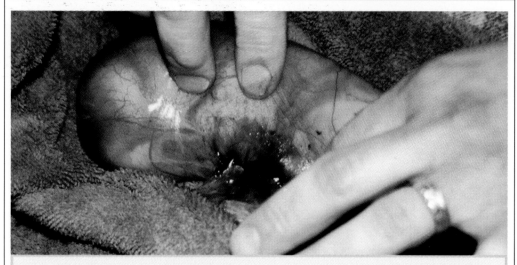

A whelp still in its sac, the dark red is part of the afterbirth attached to the umbilical cord.

about two hours, and the description that I heard went like this: "The puppies just fell out all over the place. Marsha kept saying, 'Puppy coming!' All the time, Steve was in the background droning, 'Color? Sex? Marking? Afterbirth? Weight? General Condition? No one's answering me!' For crying out loud! We didn't know if we were on puppy six or puppy ten!" So much for that whelping chart!

If all goes as above, you will have been witness to an ideal whelping. The only aid that you will have needed to give is moral support to the mother. In many breeds, this is the way whelping occurs—pups appear one after another. This is particularly true in the medium to large breeds. In the smaller breeds and the short-legged ones in particular, you will have to give a helping hand at least part of the time. With some breeds you will assist with every whelp, and you will have to have professional assistance part of the time.

ASSISTING AS EACH WHELP IS BORN

Many breeders prefer to open the sacs and cut the cords themselves. It is important that the sac be taken off the head of the pup immediately. If you do not remove the sac promptly, the puppy can suffocate because it cannot get air into its lungs. If you want to remove the sac yourself, rather than letting the bitch do it, take a quick look and determine which end of the sac contains the pup's head. Then tear the sac open, using the forefinger and the thumb of each hand. Give the pup's nose a squeeze with the thumb and forefinger. This action should cause the pup to give a cry. If it doesn't, give the nose several squeezes and put your finger in its mouth to remove any mucous. If the pup still does not cry, and if it appears to have a lot of mucous in the nasal passage, pick up the pup and the afterbirth in a towel. (Newborn pups are very slippery; a towel will help

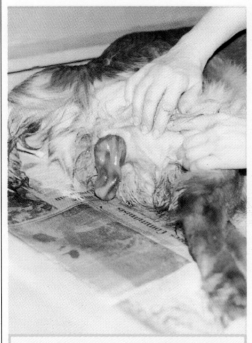

The whelp, in its sac, is just appearing. This looks like a breech presentation with the rear legs emerging first.

you to grasp the pup more securely.) Hold on to the body and the afterbirth with your left hand, *grasp the pup's head firmly* with right hand, and point the puppy's head down toward the ground. Give several good shakes of the head with the right hand as though you were shaking down a thermometer. Wipe off any mucous that has collected on the mouth and nose and repeat the process. If the pup still has not let out a squeal, rub the body well. Repeat the shaking until you hear a squeak. Once you hear a cry, you know your pup is on his way to life.

Do not worry about cutting the cord from the afterbirth. Do not worry about getting the puppy on a nipple. *Just be sure that the puppy is breathing well.* There will be plenty of time to do the rest of the chores. There is never any big hurry to either get puppies on a nipple or to cut cords. Do use haste in getting the sacs removed and getting each pup breathing.

Take a look at the umbilical cord attached to the afterbirth. You will see some veins and blood in the cord. Using your fingers, try and push this toward the pup. With a clean scissors, cut the cord two to three inches from the stomach. Do not pull the cord and risk causing a hernia. It is not necessary to tie the cord with a string. However, if the cord starts to bleed, attach your artery forceps for a few minutes. You can also sever the cord with the thumb and forefinger of each hand. The cord has a weak spot about three inches from the body, and it should sever easily at that point.

Dry the puppy with a clean towel, and give it to the mother.

The sac must be removed from the puppy's head promptly to allow the whelp to get air into his lungs. The rear of the pup is free while the head is still in the sac.

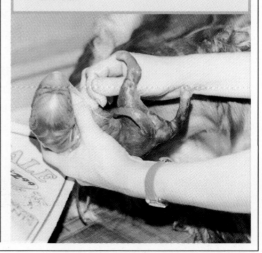

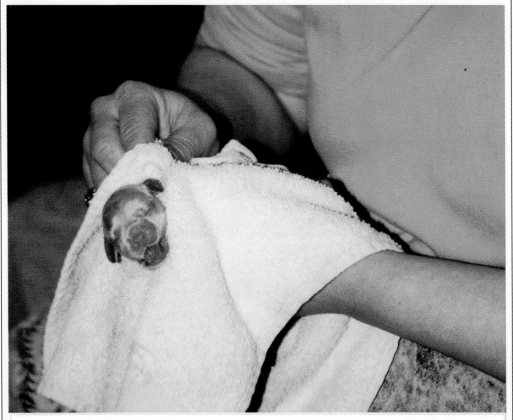

A puppy being wiped off before presented to the mother. This minutes-old pup already looks contented!

Breeders' Survey

How often do you assist the bitch with her litter and perform such activities as pulling pups, opening sacs, and cutting cords? All breeders assisted as needed with the whelpings. Note the large number that aided with each whelp.

<u>18</u> Assist with every whelping by cutting cords, pulling pups, and opening sacs. Many of the breeders opened every sac and cut all of the cords. Some just opened the sacs; and some only cut cords.

<u>4</u> Assist at least fifty percent of the time during the whelping.

<u>3</u> Seldom assist.

<u>2</u> Always have Cesarean sections.

Whelping Chart

Sire _____   Dam _____

Dates bred _____   Date whelped _____

Labor starts _____

  Hard labor starts _____

  Water bag appears _____

	Time whelped	Afterbirth	Sex	Color/Markings	Weight	OK?
Puppy 1						
Puppy 2						
Puppy 3						
Puppy 4						
Puppy 5						

Notes:

Illustration of a blank whelping chart.

ONWARD WITH THE WHELPING

It is now time to put hot water in the hot water bottle. Take water from the tap. You don't want it scalding hot; but you want it "toasty" warm. Fill the bottle about half full and "burp" it. The bottle should feel like a water bed, not a big, hot lump. Cover the bottle with a towel and place it in your towel-lined ready box. Put the lid on the box (or cover it with another towel) and you now have a cozy incubator.

Watch your mother for more signs of labor. When she begins to lose interest in her pup and starts to look restless again, take the pup away and put it in the ready box. At this point most mothers will not notice that the pup is gone. As she did earlier, your mother will strain, cry and scratch her bedding, although she now has a good idea about what is happening. Soon another whelp will appear. Follow the previously described procedures, marking the time of the birth for each pup on your chart.

Keep track of the afterbirths, and note them on your chart.

Mothers will often eat afterbirths, and this is normal, but one or two are enough. Some breeders think the placenta contains hormones that aid labor and help milk production. Others think that placentas disrupt the digestive track—and, if the mother eats five or six, they certainly will. Therefore, one or two will cause no problems, and don't worry if she doesn't eat any of them. Some bitches will look at you as though you're nuts when you offer them an afterbirth. When you look at one closely, you can't really blame them! Others will reach around and devour them so fast that you might have trouble knowing for sure if the afterbirth actually came out.

If you cannot account for an afterbirth for each pup, be sure to take your bitch to the veterinarian after the whelping has been completed. If the whelping has occurred in the evening, take her the next morning. The veterinarian will give the dam a shot of oxytocin to bring down the retained afterbirth. See a veterinarian, too, if you suspect any retained whelps after the whelping is completed. This is important, since retained afterbirths can cause problems later, and retained whelps can cause severe problems.

If, after a pup comes out, the cord breaks and the afterbirth remains in the mother, check to see whether a portion of the cord is hanging from the vulva. If it is, attach the artery forceps and *very gently* try to ease the afterbirth out of the uterus. Do not use a jerking motion; a slow, pulling motion will do. If you are unable to retrieve the afterbirth with forceps, simply wait. The retained afterbirth will sometimes come out just before the next pup is whelped. *Do not under any circumstances insert the forceps into the vulva.*

After your bitch has delivered several pups, she may appreciate some water. Bring her a pan, but don't let her "tank up" on it. Give her just enough to help her feel comfortable.

WHEN THE WHELPING IS FINISHED

You should be able to tell when your mother is finished whelping. Shortly after delivering her last whelp, she will "settle in." She will look relaxed and pleased. She has her brood around her, and she should project an air of "all's well with the world." At this point, you can stand her up on all four legs and feel the stomach area with both hands. There should be an "empty" feeling, and if there is still another pup inside you should be able to feel it. Often she will give several more pushes even though there are no more whelps to be delivered.

Give your bitch another pan of water, and, while she is drinking, put the pups in the ready box again. Take your mother outside and take along a towel in case it is needed. Let her exercise briefly and walk her around for a few minutes. Bring her back inside and get the whelping pen ready for its new function—puppy rearing.

A "from the book" whelping
(The kind you always hope to have)

Sire _Ch. Firebrand's Paymaster_   Dam _Ch. Firebrand's Fair Weather_

Dates bred _6/18, 20, 21_   Date whelped _8/22/81_

Labor starts _9:10 a.m_

Hard labor starts _____

Water bag appears _10:15 a.m._

	Time whelped	Afterbirth	Sex	Color/Markings	Weight	OK?
Puppy 1	10:25	✓	m	Black	7	
Puppy 2	10:50	✓	f	Brown	8	
Puppy 3	11:15	✓	m	Black	5½	no
Puppy 4	12:00	✓	f	Brown	7½	
Puppy 5	12:20	✓	f	Black	6½	

12:30 · All cleaned up.

Notes

Very easy litter to whelp. Pups small - all "popped" out.

Puppy 3 not breathing well.

2nd day - puppy 3 died.

5th day - all 4 pups doing fine.

3 weeks - puppies almost weaned. All up on legs, moving well. Look good.

Illustration of a successful whelping chart from an "ideal" breeding — what all breeders would like to experience!

Take out all of the dirty towels and newspapers and wipe the pen or box down with a power towel or sponge. Lay down a layer of newspapers and put a bath towel over it. This is also the time to insert the buffer rail, if it is separate from the pen.

Put the mother in the pen and place one pup at a time in the pen. Look over each pup to make sure it has four legs and two ears, and check for cleft palates. Show

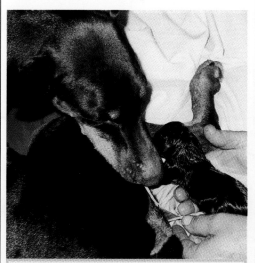

This Doberman Pinscher dam first eats the placenta, a source of many nutrients, and then cleans the pup. Breeders, Chris and Dara Swendsen.

each pup to the mother and then tuck it up to a nipple. (Now, let's use some common sense: don't start looking for your "show quality" pups at this point!)

After all the pups are in a box, and if necessary, I wrap an old bed sheet around the whelping pen to keep off any drafts. Clamp-clothespins hold the sheet in place. If the outdoor temperature is less than seventy-five degrees, clamp on the reflector lamp and

turn this on only half of the pen. If the mother becomes too warm, she will move to the darker and cooler side of the pen.

After mother and pups have settled into their clean whelping box, you will probably want to prepare a small pan of food for your bitch. For the first feeding, make the portion small and add a little cottage cheese and some canned dog food to the kibble or meal. Make the first few meals fairly mushy or soupy.

Pick up all your towels and wash them. Whelping rooms have a peculiar aroma all their own, and you will probably want to remove the odors as soon as possible. After the towels are disposed of, you may want to take a bath, have a cup of coffee or a drink, and breathe a sigh of "well done!"

WHELPING BOX ENVIRONMENT

Most books tell you to keep the whelping box at a temperature of ninety degrees for the first week. The ninety degree temperature, however, can be too much for some mothers to endure comfortably. Furthermore, this temperature level can be difficult to maintain consistently. The majority of the breeders in the survey thought that ninety degrees was too warm, and many said that they had problems with mothers becoming dehydrated. A few breeders did keep their boxes at ninety degrees for the first week, but most felt that seventy-five to eighty degrees was sufficient. However, remember that chilling—allowing the pup's body

Shaking down a puppy.

temperature to drop—is a major factor in puppy deaths.

To maintain warmth, it is best to keep the whelping box out of drafts and to use a reflector shade with a regular light bulb for additional heat. During the first week or two, turn the light on the pups whenever you take the bitch out of the pen. When she is out of the pen, you can also cover the pups with a towel or an old sweater. Of course, the problem of puppy warmth is not so crucial if you live in a warm climate. But if you live in a cold climate, and you have had a winter litter, you have to do more to keep the newborns warm when they are by themselves. During the first seven to fourteen days, your mother will get out of the box only to exercise

so she will be a great help in providing warmth.

Some veterinarians think that the use of both a heating pad or an infrared light can dehydrate pups. By using a reflector shade with a regular bulb, you should be able to avoid this problem. In addition, you can change your bulbs and use sixty or forty or twenty-five watt bulbs, depending on the degree of warmth desired. Hot water bottles are ideal, but these should be reheated every three or four hours. Some breeders use quartz heaters near the whelping box and they find these most satisfactory. Whatever you use for additional heat, follow these precautions:

1) Cover only a portion of your pen so that your mother and the

pups can get away from the heat when they want to.

2) If you have to use extension cords, be sure that they are in good condition.

3) Do not cover your bulbs or heaters with sheets, blankets, or towels. You can easily start a fire.

I use an old sweater with my pups. I have several large, washable, mohair-type cast-offs; and often it seems that the pups can't tell them from their mother. They cuddle up in the sweater, often crawling into the sleeves and preparing a little cocoon. The sweater usually stays with the litter (with some washings, of course!) until the pups are four weeks of age. A puppy with a sweater rarely gets cold. A small thermometer attached near ground level in your whelping box will give you the temperature of the box at puppy level.

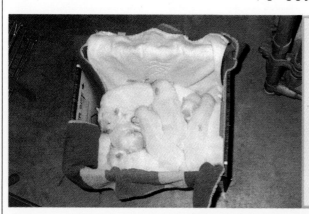

Old blankets, towels, or even an old sweater placed in their whelping box will help keep your new puppies in a warm environment. These are five-day-old Samoyed pups bred by Jim and Elfie Shea.

BREEDERS' SURVEY

Do you feel that it is necessary to keep your pups in a ninety-degree environment for the first week? Yes <u>9</u>   No <u>18</u>
Of the nine that answered "yes," three had difficulties with the bitch becoming dehydrated. Most of the breeders preferred to have the temperature around eighty degrees. One breeder said, "Are you kidding? At ninety degrees she'd be dead!"

Although infrared bulbs and heating pads can cause dehydration, they were the most popular heat sources for most of the breeders.

If you add heat to your whelping box, what do you use?

Infrared light <u>15</u>
Heating Pad <u>12</u>
Reflector Shade <u>4</u>
Quartz Heater <u>4</u>
Hot Water Bottle <u>2</u>

Several breeders used more than one source of heat—a heating pad and a reflector light, for example. *All* the breeders used some source of additional heat.

WEATHER: HOW THE HEAT AND COLD AFFECT A LITTER

It is important to keep young pups out of drafts, which can kill a litter. If you live in a warm climate where the temperature stays around seventy or eighty degrees most of the time, you will have fewer problems than if you live in the northern climates. If you live in a cold climate, do not put your pups next to a radiator to keep them warm. Use the mother's own body heat and supplement with either hot water bottles, lamps, heaters, or sweaters. There are quartz heaters on the market that aim the heat at a specific area, and many breeders find that these work well. Whatever heating element you use, spot it only on part of the pen or box so that the mother and pups can get out of the heat if they wish. If you cover your pen (if you are using a pen) with a sheet at night, the mother's body heat should keep the area warm without the use of electrical appliances. A word of warning on using any electrical appliances for warmth: be sure that extension cords are in good condition, and *do not* put any sheets or blankets over any heaters or light fixtures. The fire hazard is small, but it is a potential danger.

It is easier to have a litter when the weather is mild and dry and you are able to put your puppies outdoors at four or five weeks of age. The sunshine and

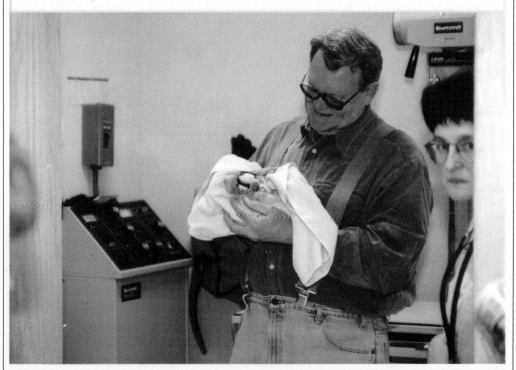

"Proud papa" Karl Dingman of Dingman's Bulldogs holds the newest addition to his canine family.

Sassy settles in after a job well done with her one-day-old pups. Owners, Jim and Elfie Shea.

outdoor exercise helps build strong bodies. Unfortunately, one cannot always pick the best weather one wants for the pups' arrival.

Extreme heat is the other end of the weather problem. If it is ninety-five degrees the day that your girl whelps, don't worry about it; you want the pups warm anyway. However, don't place the whelping pen over or near an open window, since the breeze can blow in on the young pups. Do not use a room air conditioner for the first two weeks unless you have to. Also, try to avoid using a fan. You can tell how warm your pups are by noting how far they spread out in the box. For the first two weeks, puppies usually stay close together—and close to mother. It is not unusual to look in a box the first week and not see any puppies, since they often stay underneath mother. If it is exceptionally warm, they spread out in the box. Use your common sense in this situation. If the pups are too warm to nurse, or if the mother is in distress, you will have to use an air conditioner or fan.

If the heat and humidity continue for days and mother and the pups develop problems—such as not eating or nursing—you will have to use stronger measures. To cool them, rinse out a small towel in cold water, wring it dry, and place it in the whelping box, covering only about one-quarter of the surface. Even very young pups will promptly learn that it feels good to have a cool tummy; and within a few minutes they will stretch out and go to sleep on the cloth. Rinse out the towel about four times a day and change it daily. The cool, wet cloth pulls the heat right out of the pups. If you feel that a puppy is really having a difficult time, put some cool water on its stomach. This will cause the body temperature to drop fast because the large blood vessels are close to the surface on the stomach and inner legs. I don't like to use wet cloths on litters under two weeks of age; but if the heat and humidity are severe there is not much choice. (Sometimes after leaving your little pups settled on the cloth, happily sleeping, you turn around and find that mother has pushed everyone off and is sitting enjoying the cool cloth!) If the heat becomes very severe, fill several large glass jars with cold water, put the lids on, and place them in the whelping pen. Even very young pups will gather around them to keep cool.

Remember, for heat and cold:

1) Use your common sense. Both extreme heat and extreme cold call for extra measures. You should be able to tell by looking at or feeling your puppies whether they are running into trouble.

2) Never cover the entire pen or box with either lamps or wet cloths. Cover only one-quarter or one-half of it so that the mother and pups can move to an area *away* from either the heat or wet cloths.

3) Never put a cover, like a sheet or blanket, over an electrical appliance.

SUPPLEMENTS

Many breeders surveyed use supplements. By feeding a good, balanced dog food, you should be able to provide most of a pup's nutritional needs without using supplements. Breeders of large and giant breeds often supplement at all stages, since these animals grow at a rapid rate. If you do use supplements, get them from your veterinarian and follow his instructions.

BREEDERS' SURVEY

Do you give your mothers dietary supplements while in whelp?
Yes __20__   No __6__

Do you give your mothers supplement while nursing?
Yes __20__   No __6__

If so, do you give vitamins?   __19__   calcium __7__   other __17__

Whelping Problems

Up to this point we have assumed that there are no whelping problems. Some breeders rarely, if ever, have problems, other breeders have problems fairly often. And a third group—the Brachycephalic breeds (Bulldogs, Boston Terriers, etc.)—routinely have problems and nearly always need Cesarean sections.

If this is your first litter, make it a point to read up on your breed to determine whether whelping problems are common. Also talk to other breeders in the area and find out what kind of problems they have experienced with the breed. If an old-time breeder of twenty years experience rarely has had a whelping problem, the chances are very good that you will not have one either. (Remember to talk to someone who is open and who is willing to help newcomers.)

Some Broad Generalizations:

1) The larger the breed, the fewer the problems.

2) The more overweight the mother, the greater the chance for problems.

3) The longer the leg on the breed, the fewer the problems; conversely, the shorter the leg, the greater the problems.

4) The larger the head in proportion to the body on the breed, the more problems.

Newborn puppies are extremely vulnerable and certain breeds need extra care in order to assure that all goes well during delivery. Labrador Retrievers are among the most hardy of all pups.

5) The larger the whelp, the greater the chance for problems.

6) The older the mother, the greater the chance for problems.

The Most Common Causes of Whelping Problems:

1) An extra large whelp.

2) Incorrect presentation of the whelp into the birth canal.

3) Uterine inertia.

4) Long delay between the delivery of pups.

All four of these problems can overlap. A malpresentation or an extra large pup can cause a long delay in delivery. Uterine inertia can be caused by a long delay due to either a large or a poorly presented whelp.

In this manual I have tried to cover most of the problems that you may experience. Don't become alarmed as you read. Most deliveries are problem-free, but you should be prepared to know when a problem is developing. A puppy or two saved can pay your stud fee or shipping costs—or can pay for a Cesarean section.

LABOR STARTS AND A WHELP DOES NOT APPEAR

Your bitch began labor at twelve noon. She has been consistently having strong contractions, but it is one-thirty and still no puppy has appeared. At this point, put her leash on and take her out for a short walk (taking along a towel just in case) around the back yard. Put her back in the whelping box and watch for any action.

It is now two-thirty. Two and one-half hours have elapsed since labor began, and you still do not have a puppy. Call your veterinarian and tell him exactly what has occurred. Usually he will tell you to wait another half-hour or so and then bring your bitch in—or

---

BREEDERS' SURVEY

How often do you have major whelping problems that require the assistance of a veterinarian?

100%—Two breeders with Bulldogs, which almost always require Cesarean sections.

75%—One breeder with a Toy breed

25% to 30%—Six breeders

15% to 20%—Twelve breeders

Never—Three breeders

Note that fifteen breeders, slightly over half, have never—or almost never—had problems. Three of the breeders have breeds that routinely experience problems. That leaves ten breeders in a rather gray area: they may or may not have problems—that is, they may experience problems between fifteen and thirty percent of the time.

If you are faced with a large whelp in a breech position that is not going anywhere, you may have to gently pull the pup out by the rear legs.

call him back. By placing this call, you have alerted your veterinarian that there might be a problem. Usually your bitch will expel a puppy within three hours from the onset of labor. (For some reason, the call to the veterinarian often seems to provoke some action.) Once the first puppy is whelped, the birth canal is well dilated, and most of your problems are over. Veterinarians almost always want to wait three hours between the delivery of pups—or between the onset of labor and the whelping of the first pup—before being asked to assist.

A LARGE WHELP

Sometimes a puppy emerges half way—and is not going anywhere. This can more often happen in small breeds when the whelp is large. Give the mother an opportunity to expel the whelp on her own. It may take four or five contractions before it emerges. Do not panic, although you are entitled to do some hand-wringing.

If the sac is still intact and if there is a normal presentation (head first), you are in good shape, and you can give your bitch a little time to work the pup out. If it is a breech birth (rear first), do not delay beyond a few strong contractions; and then try to get the puppy out, using one or all of the following methods:

1) Stand the bitch up on all four legs or turn her over on her other side. Occasionally this change of position will cause the whelp to pop out.

2) Wash your hands well and stand the bitch up in the whelping box. Put some petroleum jelly or other lubricant on your index

finger and run your finger around between the pup and the vulva. Try to determine if the pup is caught on anything. Grasp the puppy with a towel and try to rotate the pup gently to the right—and then to the left. Do not break the sac while rotating. Let your bitch have a few more contractions and then see if your actions have helped any. Run your finger between the pup and the vulva again and, again, try to gently rotate the pup to the right and to the left.

3) Place your bitch on a table and have an assistant hold her head to keep her from snapping at you. Using a clean, small towel, firmly grip the pup with your right hand. When the bitch has a contraction, pull the pup gently and steadily downward toward the bitch's rear legs. You should pull with the contractions. With your left hand, push the vulva up towards her back. Also, again try to rotate the pup. Usually this kind of problem is a breech presentation. Therefore, you will be working with the rear end and the rear legs. Sometimes your bitch will not be having any contractions, but still the pup has to come out. With your towel in your hand, grasp the puppy and apply slow, steady pressure in a downward direction.

If you are whelping by yourself, have a table cleared. Put your bitch on the table and muzzle her with a nylon stocking. If you have a grooming table with a hanger or a noose, use this equipment. Continue to pull downward with the contractions, running your

finger around the vaginal opening as you continue to work the pup loose. Occasionally there may not be any contractions. Keep pulling steadily and slowly downward. The pup has to come out eventually no matter how unpleasant the passage.

Once the pup is out, go to work on it immediately. Do not wait for the mother to do anything. Get the sac off the puppy's head, squeezing the nose and rubbing the body to get the pup breathing. Shake the pup down. The pup has come through a severe shock. It has been in the birth canal too long, and its lungs have been squeezed while stuck in the vaginal opening. Chances are that this pup may not survive.

PRESENTATION OF THE WATERBAG ONLY

Sometimes the waterbag appears but does not break and nothing more happens. After a half-hour it begins to dry up, although it stills hangs from the uterus. By now it begins to look like a balloon that is losing air. If this should happen, give your veterinarian a call and find out what to do next.

APPEARANCE OF THE HEAD ONLY

Sometimes only the head will appear. After several more contractions the puppy still will not have moved. Take the sac away from the head so that the pup can breathe, even if the ribs are still caught in the vagina. Take the first two fingers of either hand, place them behind the pup's ear on the neck, and pull down with the next contraction. As usual, use a steady, down-pulling action. You can usually pull the puppy out.

DIGITAL EXAMINATION OF THE BITCH

Sometimes it will be necessary for you to make a digital examination of your bitch. You should do this when you think that things are not going right with the whelping.

Muzzle your bitch if you are alone and wash your hands well with soap and water and rinse and dry them. Use a surgical glove if one is available. An examination can be conducted, however, without a glove. Your fingernails should be cut short and smooth. Put petroleum jelly on your index finger and insert it carefully into the vaginal opening, feeling for a pup. You should be able to insert your entire finger unless a pup is in the way. In so doing, you can ascertain where the pup is—or isn't. And you can determine if it has entered the birth canal or not.

I do a digital examination after the bitch has been in good labor for two hours and has not produced a whelp. If I can feel a pup, I wait another fifteen minutes and examine her again before I call the veterinarian. Then I can say, "She's been in labor for two and one-half hours. I did a digital exam at two hours, and I could feel a pup at the end of my finger. I examined her again right before calling you and the pup is still in the same place." This kind of information will help your veterinarian help you, and it will help him determine whether or not you should come to the office.

If only a head appears, you may have to gently assist the pup out by the head and neck.

Sometimes you will see a bulge between the vulva and the tail. If you place your fingers on this bulge, you will know that it is a pup. At this point it has passed at least half-way over the pelvic brim and it should come out shortly.

You must use your common sense in dealing with these problems. Trust your intuition. You know your bitch, and you are watching her closely. Call the veterinarian if your intuition tells you that things are not going well.

If you expect any problems at all with your whelping, you must have the assistance of a good veterinarian. Work with one that you know and trust and who is familiar with your bitch. Be sure you know his office hours. If he is not available in the evenings or on weekends, have the number of an emergency service in your area. Work around your veterinarian's hours as much as possible. If he closes at 8:00 in the evening and if at 7:45 you are one and one-half hours into what you think might be a problem, call him before he leaves for home. Many veterinarians will stay around for a half-hour or so if they think that you will need them. A veterinarian who knows you may give you his home telephone number in case you need emergency help.

When there is a long period between pups—or a lack of labor—and your bitch is periodically having good contractions, your veterinarian will probably want you to come in so that he can administer a short of oxytocin. These shots will either get labor going again or else will produce strong contractions.

PRESENTATION OF THE WHELP IN THE BIRTH CANAL

Normal presentation of a whelp is with the head first, spine facing up. In a posterior presentation, the feet will come first with the spine facing up. Sometimes one foot only will appear, and you will have to carefully work the second leg down by gently inserting your finger into the vagina and carefully pulling the foot into the proper position.

A breech presentation is when the rear (or rump) presents itself first, with the front and rear legs tucked to the body. Breech births and posterior presentations are not unusual and should not be looked at with alarm.

MALPRESENTATION

1) The puppy is presented upside down with the stomach pressing up against the roof of the pelvis. The pup is either in head first position or a breech position and, as the mother strains, the pup continues to be pushed up toward the pelvic roof.

2) The head is turned and the neck, or possibly the back, is trying to go through the birth canal. This puppy is being presented at its widest part, with the back or neck being presented first and the head and four legs following.

3) Two whelps are presented at the same time.

These are all conditions that you will probably not be able to detect yourself, and you will likely need some kind of veterinary assistance. Sometimes these pups can be pushed back into the birth canal and repositioned. Unless you are an experienced whelper, this procedure is one that your veterinarian will have to perform. Sometimes your veterinarian will be able to reposition a pup with forceps, and sometimes the bitch will have to undergo a Cesarean section. Shots of oxytocin will not alleviate these conditions and can be harmful if given at this point.

UTERINE INERTIA

This problem seems to be more common in the smaller, short-legged breeds. The problem can be caused by a large whelp that takes some time to deliver, a poorly presented whelp, a lazy bitch—or a bitch who does not want to "get hurt." Uterine inertia is also more common in older dams and in out-of-condition bitches.

With uterine inertia there will be few or no contractions for long periods of time. If your bitch had been having good labor —but no whelping has taken place—and you fail to observe a contraction in the period of an hour, call the veterinarian and make plans to take her into the office. The bitch will either have to have oxytocin administered to get labor going again, or she will have to have a Cesarean section.

IN CLOSING

I want to mention again that these problems are not common ones for most breeds, but you should be aware that the problems do exist and that the pups can be saved with your assistance or that of a veterinarian. Keep in mind that most veterinarians will want to wait close to three hours between pups, or after the onset of labor, before they consider most problems to be serious.

A last observation: if problems occur, don't fear for the bitch's life. It's my impression that bitches in whelp die about as often as women in the middle of delivery. With good supervision and a healthy bitch, death is a rare event. Do be concerned about losing pups, though, and try to take the best action possible to save their lives.

BREEDERS' SURVEY

What kind of problems do you call the veterinarian for?

Prolonged labor   15
Uterine inertia   10
Malpresentation   5
Water bag presented and no puppy   2

Whelping charts for whelping problems

Labor starts _3 p.m_

      Hard labor starts _Never_

      Water bag appears _Never_

6 p.m. - Called Vet. said to wait one hour
Never labored much. Uterine inertia?
Don't want to lose any pups in this
    litter. Skipped waiting with oxytocin.
7 p.m. - Caesarian section - all pups ok.

* *

Labor starts _3:45 a.m_

      Hard labor starts _4:55 a.m_

      Water bag appears _6:00 a.m - No pups_

Talked with Dr. Cutler at 9 a.m.
Section at 10 a.m.
One large 10½ oz. female
Pup died at one week

* *

Labor starts _10:15 a.m_

      Hard labor starts _11:30 a.m_

      Water bag appears _____

No pups by 1:45. Shot of oxytocin at Vets'.
Still good labor, but no pups.
3 p.m. Caesarian section; 4 pups (3M.2F)
    All 9-10 oz. Pups very slow and
    given a shot of B12.
1 week - All pups fine.

Whelping problems noted on whelping chart.

When to Have a Cesarean Section

Many years ago Cesarean sections were usually risky, often endangering the life of the bitch. Nowadays the risk is very slight and the operation is quick and safe. Your veterinarian should make the decision about whether your bitch requires a section. But here are some general guidelines that will help you assist in making the decision.

1) Your breed—a Bulldog, for example—routinely requires a section in almost all whelpings. The only exception usually occurs when the bitch comes from a free whelping line. If you want to chance a natural whelping, let your veterinarian know so that he will be prepared to deal with any problems.

2) Your bitch has been in hard labor for three hours, and nothing has happened. She has had one shot of oxytocin; another forty-five minutes has lapsed, and still no pups have appeared. She probably needs a section.

3) Your bitch has delivered two pups naturally, but three hours have gone by with intermittent labor—and no more pups. Your veterinarian will possibly administer one shot of oxytocin, perhaps a second shot, and then he will perform a section if there still has been no action. (In instances 2 and 3, you must keep in mind that your bitch could deliver up to six pups. She has already expended four hours or so in labor with no, or few, results. When she finally begins or resumes delivering, she will probably have another two to four hours of work ahead of her. Can she physically hold up long enough to deliver another three or four pups?)

4) Your bitch has had about a half-hour of strong labor. Three hours have passed, and either nothing has happened or the contractions have been very sporadic and weak. At this time, she may or may not have had one or two pups earlier. You have taken her for a short walk, given her some water, and encouraged her—all with no results. She is sitting in the corner of her box casting rather smug looks in your direction. You know that she has more pups to deliver, but she shows no sign of cooperating. This is called "packing it in"—or uterine inertia. If it occurs, call your veterinarian and take your bitch in. He may or may not want to try one shot of oxytocin. Do not let this problem linger too long before seeking the assistance of a veterinarian, particularly if you think that there is more than one pup yet to be delivered. Go for the section.

5) Your bitch is in obvious distress probably due to malpresentation of a whelp, and

your veterinarian says that he wants to do a section. Follow his advice.

6) Your bitch has delivered four pups and has had an additional two hours of labor. She appears to have one pup remaining to be delivered. Call the veterinarian and ask if he wants to see her. He will probably give her a shot of oxytocin. Try to avoid a section in this case.

In general, if I feel that I can save one or two pups, I will go with a section. Remember, one pup saved pays for the cost of the operation.

EMERGENCY VETERINARY SERVICE

You should know your veterinarian's hours—and whether he is on call during the night and on weekends. Many larger cities now have an emergency veterinary service that the area doctors use. This is very handy because it provides assurance that someone is available to handle problems regardless of the time of the day or the day of the week. Know the telephone number and location of the service. Even if you are not immediately whelping a litter, dogs can develop strange problems; and they often develop them at strange hours.

You should understand by now that if you have any kind of major problem in your whelping you will need professional assistance. Let's assume that you have a purebred bitch, perhaps a champion. You may have sent her halfway across the country to be bred, so not only do you have a stud fee involved but possibly large transportation costs too. If a handler is handling the stud dog, you may have an additional fee involved. Now, you already have a lot of

---

BREEDERS' SURVEY

What percentage of your litters are born by Cesarean section?

100%	2	35%	2	0% to 5%	15
75%	1	25%	2		
50%	1	10%	2		

Of this group, five never had a section, and eleven have had at least one. Eight breeders had direct experience with Cesarean sections ranging from 10 percent to 75 percent of the time. This is the group that has the greatest whelping challenge before them, since they are not sure whether or not they will have problems until the activity begins. Two breeders anticipate sections with every whelping. Fifteen breeders, over 50 percent, do not plan to have any problem, and only four of these have had to have a section at some time.

With three exceptions, breeders whose bitches have had Cesarean sections have assisted the veterinarian. If your veterinarian will allow you to assist in rubbing down the puppies, do not pass up this experience.

money in the breeding, so you do not want to take a chance losing all or part of the litter. Have the number of an available veterinary service handy, and be prepared. It seems as though problems rarely appear on weekday mornings, but they have a tendency to happen at midnight on Saturday.

One last note on emergency veterinary services. They are expensive, since they offer a specialized service not unlike calling a plumber at midnight. Be ready to write a check for the services when rendered. Some will accept major credit cards, and most will tell you when you call that you must "bring money."

A NOTE ON TRAVELING TO THE VETERINARIAN

In case of an emergency, *always call* the veterinarian first. Don't simply appear on his doorstep with your problem. By calling first, you know that he is available and that he will be prepared to deal with your specific problem.

Place your bitch in a box or a crate in the car. Keep her confined, as you do not want her "flying" around inside the car—a potential hazard to her and to you. After all, you are coping with a major problem, and you are nervous enough as it is! Take along some towels and scissors in case they are needed, and take your ready box together with an empty hot water bottle. Grab a book so that you have something to read if you have to spend several hours in the waiting room. Drive fast (but not too fast) and pray that she does not deliver any

puppies along the way! No bitch of mine has ever delivered in the car, although I always worried about the possibility.

My favorite trip to the emergency veterinarian: a friend's bitch has been in labor for *hours* and has produced one pup. At 1:00 A.M. she calls and asks if I will come over and check out the bitch. My friend, Fran, has now been up for two nights, and she can hardly move. I take her and the bitch to the emergency service, where they keep the bitch for a section. Traveling back to Fran's house at 2:00 A.M. through an undesirable section of town, I stop at a stop light. Suddenly a car whizzes by, runs the red light, hits a car from the other direction, pushes that car through a drug store window, spins around and zips by us in the opposite direction. *Well!* We were simply stunned, and the adrenaline was really racing. It took Fran days to recover from that whelping; she refused to whelp any more litters; and I midwifed the next whelping.

WHAT IS A CESAREAN SECTION?

In a Cesarean section (also called C-section), the veterinarian makes an incision in the abdomen and removes the whelps. In advance of the surgery, the veterinarian will administer an anesthetic. When your bitch becomes drowsy, he will lay her on her back on the operating table and tie all four legs down. He will then shave her stomach and prep her for the operation. A midline incision will then be made just large enough to enable him to pull out the uterus, which he lays on the bitch's stomach and rear legs. If you have not observed a Cesarean, you will marvel at nature's work, and you will wonder how that fat "sausage"— and that's what the uterus looks like when filled with puppies— could have fit into the stomach.

Note: Some veterinarians will not allow you to assist with or observe a Cesarean. Emergency services are particularly strict about this. However, your regular veterinarian usually will let you help, and quite often he will need your assistance, as it takes two or three people to get the pups going.

As each pup is removed from the uterus and the sac, it is handed to an assistant who rubs the pup with a towel to get it going. The afterbirth is still attached, and the assistant must take care not to drop it. Veterinarians will not detach the afterbirths until they have finished all their work on the bitch. When all of the pups have been removed,

the uterus is put back into the stomach, the abdominal wall sutured and the skin incision sutured. The veterinarian will usually work quickly, as he does not want to keep the bitch under the anesthetic any longer than necessary. When the veterinarian finishes his work on the bitch, he will cut the umbilical cords and examine each pup.

Prepare the ready box for the trip home. Fill the hot water bottle and place it in the box together with some towels. Place your pups in the box and cover the top with a lid or another towel. (If you have forgotten a hot water bottle, fill a surgical glove with warm water and fasten the top of it securely. The glove will look and feel like a big, warm udder, but it will do the job for you.) Wrap a towel around the rear of your bitch, since the hindquarters will be quite messy. Carry her to the car, and put her in the crate or box. The pups do not need to travel with her on the way home.

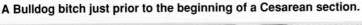

A Bulldog bitch just prior to the beginning of a Cesarean section.

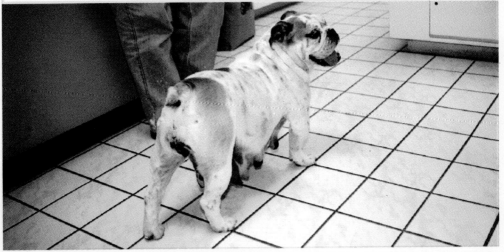

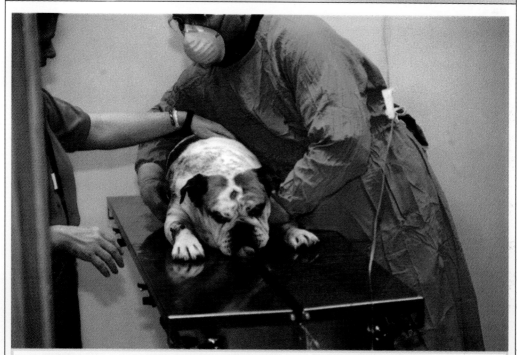

The veterinarian is carefully placing the mother on the operating table.

The incision has been made and the veterinarian is beginning the serious work.

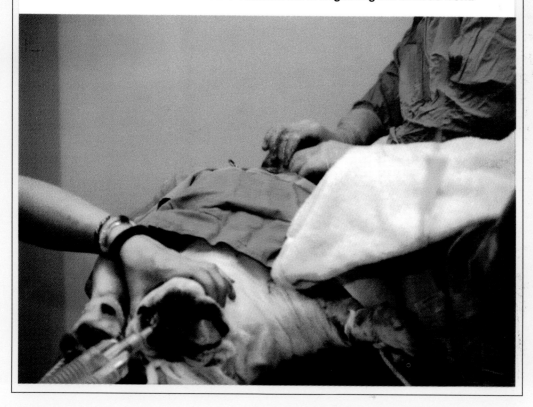

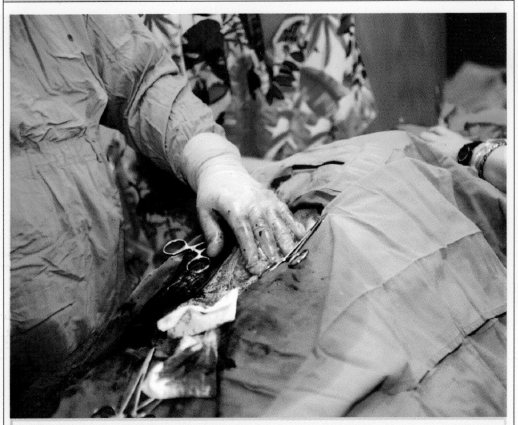

Getting ready for the first pup.

A puppy comes into the world! God and Mother Nature at their best.

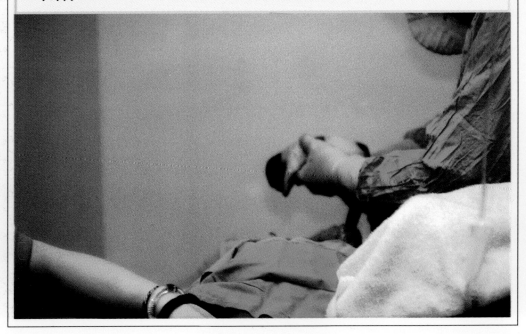

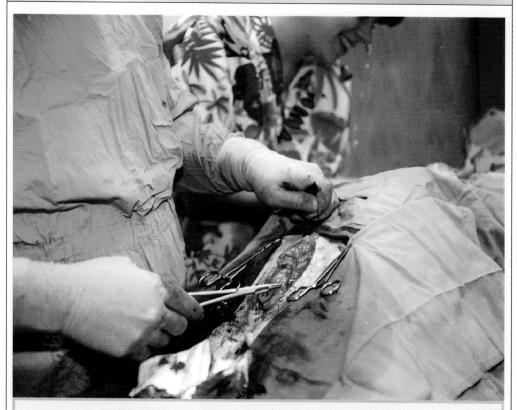

The veterinarian prepares to sew up the incision.

Surgery nearly completed.

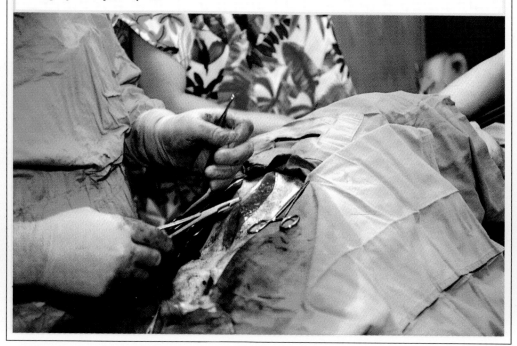

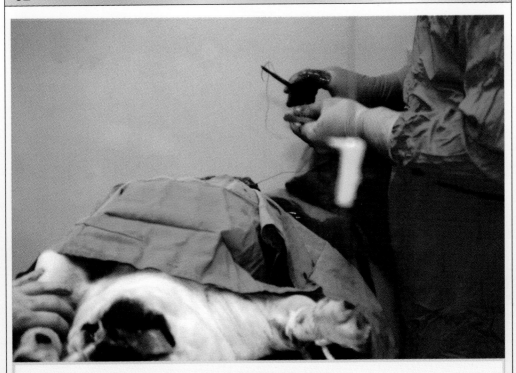

Finishing the job. Note that her legs are tied to the table.

Sutured up, cleaned up and ready to go.

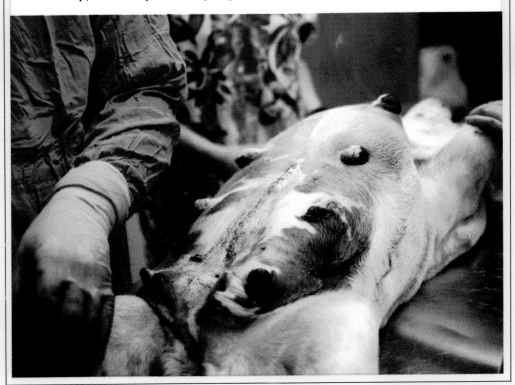

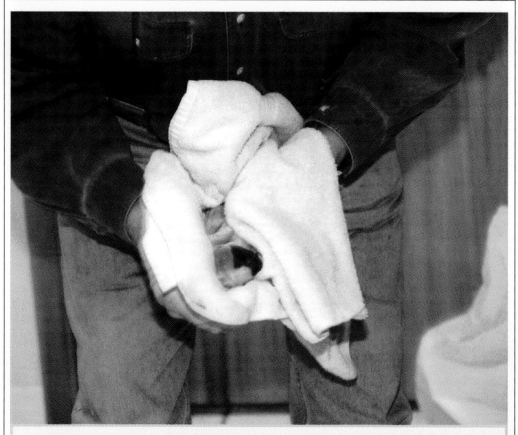

A happy breeder drying off a healthy new pup.

ACCEPTING THE PUPS AFTER A CESAREAN SECTION

You are now home, and your whelping box is cleaned up as it would be if you had had a litter normally. If this is the bitch's first litter and if it was a section, chances are good that your bitch will have some problems accepting the pups—at least for the first thirty-six hours. Remember:

1) She is very groggy and still tranquilized.

2) She has had major surgery, and she probably does not feel well.

3) She has a batch of squirming pups, and she is not sure just what they are, since she is still tranquilized.

If your mother has previously had a litter of puppies and her second or third litter requires a section, she should accept the pups readily. If your mother delivered and nursed one or two pups and *then* had the section, there may be little problem in getting her to accept the pups. The problem of the mother accepting the pups will generally arise when the first-time mother has all of her pups by Cesarean. If there is a problem and since she is still tranquilized for the first twenty-four to thirty-six hours, you may wish to take the pups from her when they are not nursing.

GETTING MOTHER AND THE PUPS SETTLED IN

1) Get your mother settled in the whelping box or pen.

2) Show her one puppy and let her sniff both the front and the back end. I generally show the mother the rear first. If she should snap, she is less likely to damage the rear than the head.

3) Carefully lay your mother on her side and put the pup on a all pups are with her. Watch them all very carefully. If your mother nuzzles the pups and tries to tuck them up to her belly, you are home free.

If the mother snaps at a puppy or continues to move away from it (I even had a mother urinate on a pup), you have a temporary crisis. When this happens, the first problem to address is yourself. You are tired out; you have prob-

After the dam is settled in the whelping box, lay her on her side and attach a pup to her nipple. As long as the mother accepts the pup and shows no adverse reaction, continue until all her pups are nursing.

nipple. You may have to open the pup's mouth and actually attach it to the nipple. Do not worry if he does not take hold immediately. If the mother shows no adverse reaction, do the same with the second puppy and continue until ably had a long night or day; you are dirty and smelly. When the mother snaps at her pups, your nerves will really get frazzled, and you will be ready to pack your suitcase. Have hope. This problem will last about thirty hours—until

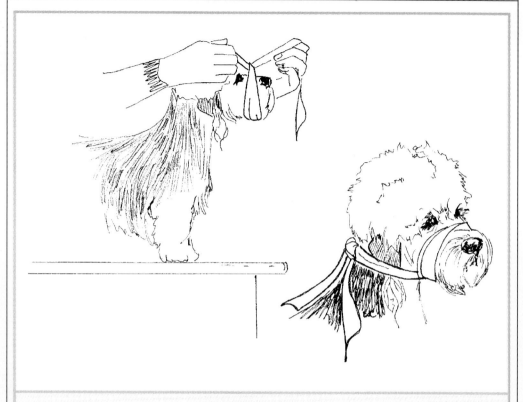

An illustration of how to muzzle your dog.

the tranquilizer wears off—and you will just have to hold on.

If you do not trust the mother, put the pups on her about every three or four hours and keep them in the ready box the rest of the time. You may have to hold the mother's head the first time or two that the pups nurse, but after a few nursings you should be able to merely sit close by and observe. Watch her mouth to see if she is curling her lip. If so, put your hand on her head or shoulders so that you can control her in case she snaps. Be sure to separate the mother from the pups when you are not in attendance. During this period, feed the mother by herself—not with the pups. Young pups do not nurse continually

since they spend approximately ninety percent of their time sleeping. If you put the pups next to her every three or four hours during the day, you can go six hours during the night and get yourself some sleep.

If the mother is not cleaning the pups during the first thirty-six hours, you will have to do so. The mother's licking stimulates the pups to urinate and defecate. You may have to help out by rubbing the pup's belly and anal region until she is ready to take on her motherly chores.

A while ago I whelped a litter for a friend. It was a first litter, and the bitch had uterine inertia, which requires a section. When I brought her home that evening, she snapped at her pups. For the next twenty-four hours I kept the pups in the whelping pen and put the mother in a crate next to the pen (which she thought was just fine); and I held her down for nursing. The second morning she awakened me with her barking. I knew that she was ready for the pups. I ran downstairs and dropped her in the pen, hardly giving them a second glance for the next two weeks. She turned out to be a Super Mom. (Note: A Super Mom is like the Super Bowl—the first letters are in caps whether written or spoken. A popular phrase: "She is a Super Mom." Friends tell you about their Super Moms when you are suffering along with a not-so-Super Mom.)

Not all bitches will be reluctant to accept the pups after a section.

About fifty percent of those having their first litter will be reluctant mothers. Do not give up the ship. Acceptance will come in a matter of hours.

If your bitch had to have a Cesarean, you should check her incision each day. Be sure that it is clean and that all sutures are holding. If you see a sign of infection, call your veterinarian. The stitches are removed about ten days after the operation.

A side note: I find that pups born by section are in much better shape at birth than those born naturally. The sectioned pups are round and fat, and they seem to gain weight a bit more quickly. Perhaps their energies go immediately into developing, since they do not have to experience the trauma of natural birth.

BREEDERS' SURVEY

Have you had any difficulty with mothers not accepting their pups after a Cesarean section?

Yes _9_   No _14_

What do you do with the problem?

Most waited it out and assisted the pups with nursing. Some separated the pups and the dam. And a few slept in the same room for the first night or two.

Let us now get back to the natural whelping. I hope you have been guided through any problems that may come up with the whelping. The pups are now into the world, but just barely. Now we need to discuss the next step: getting the pups out of the sac.

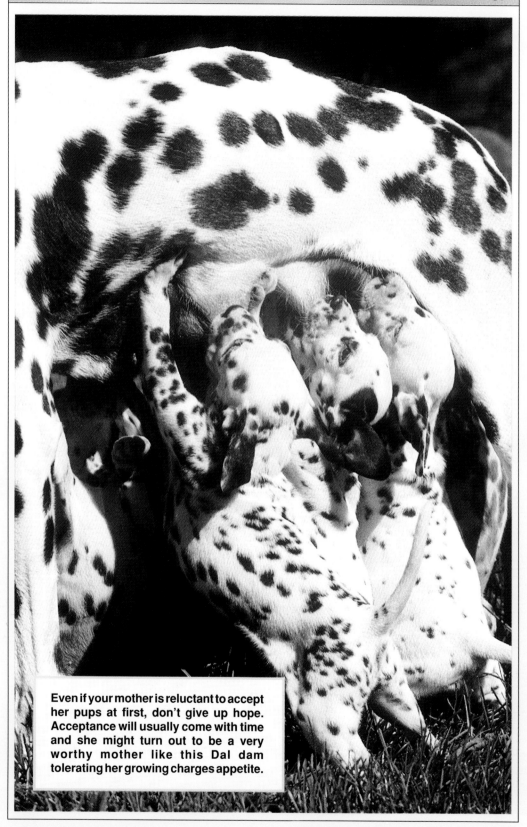

Even if your mother is reluctant to accept her pups at first, don't give up hope. Acceptance will usually come with time and she might turn out to be a very worthy mother like this Dal dam tolerating her growing charges appetite.

Newborn Pups

Immediately after the puppy has been whelped, give it a good rubbing with a Turkish towel. Use a hand towel or something smaller than a bath towel so that you do not lose the pup in a mass of material. Use some discretion in your rubbing; rub well but not so vigorously that you injure the pup. Once the pup is fairly dry and is making noises, weigh it and give it to the mother. The mother will usually nuzzle it around, wash it again, and then draw it up toward her breasts. My mothers always have a great curiosity about the cord, and they wash it very thoroughly.

SLOW STARTING PUPS

You may have a difficult birth— one that requires considerable time. The pup does not respond to a nose squeeze, but is still warm, and it has a pink tongue. Go to work on this pup immediately. It is often possible to revive a seem- ingly dead pup even fifteen min- utes after delivery. You should work on all pups that "look dead" for anywhere from two to fifteen minutes. If a pup comes out with an obvious physical deformity, and if it appears dead, there is no point in working on it. If the pup feels cold and has a gray tongue and a head that lops to the side, spend just enough time on it to make sure that there is no life. The pink-tongued, inactive pups are the ones that require quick and firm action. They are the ones most likely to be saved.

WHAT TO DO WITH A SLOW STARTING PUP

Take this pup from the mother immediately and give it a good, brisk rubbing with the towel to help get the circulation going. Hold the pup in the towel with its stomach in the palm of one hand. Rub in a back and forth motion with the towel as though you were polishing a shoe. While doing this, give the pup some nose squeezes and watch for any signs of life. As noted earlier, hold the pup firmly in your right hand with the head between your thumb and index finger and shake it to remove any mucous. Hold the pup to your ear and listen for any sounds. Once you hear a cry, you can bet that the road to life is more or less straight ahead.

If after this assistance your pup still has not come around, firmly hold the head in the towel (head pointing down) between both hands. Hold the pup above your head, and then swing your arms down in an arc between your knees, giving the pup a bit of a shake at the bottom of the swing. Try this several times, and, if this does not work, hold the pup in your right hand and again shake it. Give more nose squeezes.

Again put the puppy to your ear and listen for sounds of life. Do not worry about harming the

Swinging a slow-starting pup.

puppy. If you don't take any kind of emergency action, the pup will die. You have nothing to lose. Keep in mind that your chances of saving a pup in trouble lessen with each passing moment.

Hold the pup upside down by its rear legs so that the abdomen falls toward the lungs. (You are holding the puppy by his rear legs, head hanging down.) Hold the pup by the shoulder again and tip the pup right side up. Do this about twenty times.

Try some artificial respiration. Lay the pup on his back, open his mouth, and pull the tongue forward with your finger. Slowly press the chest walls with the thumb and index finger. Then release the pressure and let the chest expand to let the air come out. (This last action can be deceiving. Filling the lungs with air can cause one to falsely be-

lieve that something is happening.) Try this resuscitation technique about ten times.

In between all these measures, rub the pup briskly. If the tongue keeps getting grayer, you are fighting a losing battle.

Keep a towel handy for working with the puppy while you are performing these life-saving efforts. The pup is small, wet and slippery; and you can easily lose your grip and drop it. (Worse yet, swing it across the room!)

As a last resort, dab a bit of brandy or bourbon on the pup's nose and tongue. This will have the same effect as smelling salts. (A favorite whelping story: a friend is whelping pups in the bedroom while her husband is sleeping. She's been working for a while on a lifeless pup and she calls out: "Ed! Quick! Run downstairs and get me a jigger of brandy!" Ed jumps out of bed from a sound

The breeder is clearing the mucus out of the puppy's mouth. Note how the breeder is holding the head firmly between her fingers.

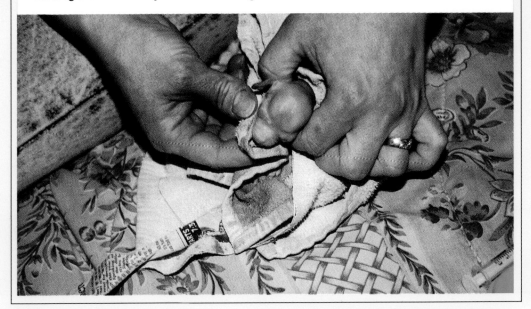

sleep and says, "Do you want that with soda or on the rocks?")

Of all these measures, I prefer the quick shake—the technique that is similar to shaking a thermometer. If the puppy is reason-

Remember to watch the tongue: pink is good, and gray is certainly bad. Listen to the pup. Hold its body to your ear and listen for any signs of life. If the head lops over to the side, you probably

Tipping a pup.

ably strong, I find that this action usually brings him around quickly. Artificial respiration and the swinging of the pup do not seem to get as good or as immediate a reaction. However, when trying to save a pup, try all measures.

I would not bother to work on a pup for longer than fifteen minutes. If the pup is strong, it will survive. Sometimes when you manage to save a pup through heroic efforts, it up and dies a week later after you have struggled for days.

have a dead puppy. You may not agree, but not all pups are meant to live—or should live. Mother Nature really does know best.

HOW TO TELL THE BOYS FROM THE GIRLS

I am always a little surprised when people cannot tell the boy pups from the girl pups. I know of several new breeders who have had this problem. ("We had two boys and three girls." Two weeks later they suddenly have four boys and one girl.) Recently I heard of some senior veterinary

Trixie, a Toy Fox Terrier, with her three-day-old puppies owned by Sherry Baker Scott.

students who told a breeder, "You have five boys." Two hours later: "Sorry, we made a mistake. You have four girls and one boy." (The breeder was so frazzled at this point that she didn't know whether she should laugh or cry.) It's really discouraging when senior veterinary students can't tell the boys from the girls. To test all of this further, I showed a pup to my mother who had lived seventy-some years, and *she* couldn't tell which was which.

Just a reminder: the girls have their "plumbing" between their rear legs and the boys have theirs in the middle of the stomach. Umbilical cords hanging down are just that. Don't confuse them with penises.

GOOD MOTHERS (OR SUPER MOMS)

Most bitches are good mothers; you will rarely have a poor mother. Some mothers are Super Moms, and this is what you would like to have. The breeders' survey produced some interesting responses to questions about the qualities of mothers. All the breeders had had good mothers— and many had had Super Moms. In general, all felt that a good mother will produce daughters who in turn will be good mothers. Likewise, I have found that good whelpers will produce daughters that are good whelpers.

Many breeders said that keeping the pups clean was a prime quality of motherhood. It takes time to clean a litter, and it is discouraging to have mother sit by and watch you do all of the work. Some mothers will not show any interest in the rear end of the pup. (Obviously not a Super Mom.)

Next to good cleaning habits, the breeders like to see calmness

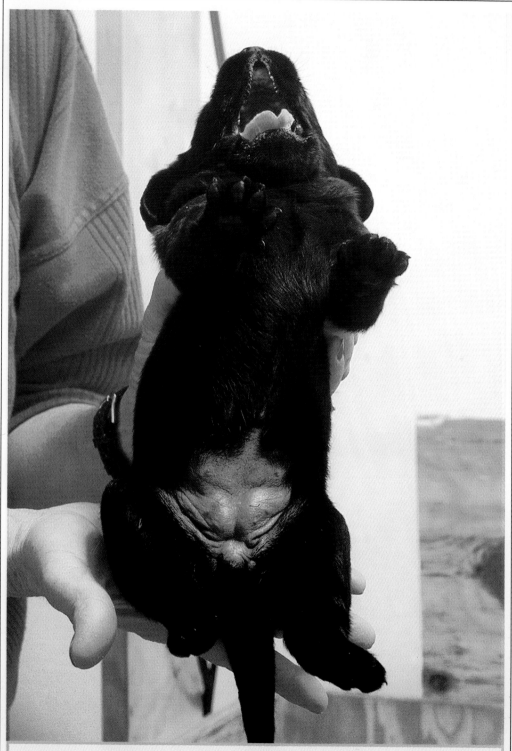

Sometimes it can be difficult to tell the difference between the boys and the girls in a litter. This is a female Labrador Retriever at three weeks of age. Breeder, Emily Magnani.

in a mother and a willingness to share the pups with their human family. An overly protective mother is unpleasant to have around. If she growls and grabs your hand when you put it in the box, you should give her a good slap and a *"no."* Get that problem cleared up immediately. Always be careful when you have strangers in to see the pups. Do not let them put their hands in the pen. If you have young children in the home, tell them that they cannot have their friends in to see the pups unless you are in the room. The last thing you need at this time is to have a neighbor's child bitten by a protective mother.

A bouncy mother can cause a bit of concern, and she certainly raises some good, tough pups. This is the mother who at the drop of a hat or the click of the toaster jumps up and hangs over the pen to see what is happening.

She spends a lot of time hanging over her pen, observing life on the "outside," and her pups spend a lot of time getting bounced off the nipples and jumped upon—a noisy group all in all. I have had a fair share of this type of mother and there is nothing one can do to change her ways. Bouncy mothers also have bouncy daughters. The best attitude for a good mother is summed up by one breeder: "A common sense approach to life."

Occasionally you will read about cannibalism in mothers, and you may hear some grim stories. Cannibalism is extremely rare. In the breeders' survey, it occurred only twice in over one thousand litters. On the few occasions when it does happen, I believe that it is the result of an inexperienced and overly protective mother who becomes frightened. Do not worry about cannibalism; it rarely happens.

BREEDERS' SURVEY

What traits do you like to see in good mother?
Remains calm and careful <u>16</u>
Keeps pups clean <u>14</u>
Shows devotion <u>10</u>
Is somewhat protective (but not overly protective) <u>9</u>
Is willing to nurse <u>5</u>
Is trusting <u>5</u>
(I liked this comment: "Quiet dignity.")
Have most of your mothers been good mothers?
All breeders answered "yes."

If you have had a good whelper and a good mother, do you find that the majority of her female offspring are the same way?
Yes <u>21</u>   **No** <u>3</u>

DEFECTIVE PUPS

Once in a great while your bitch will deliver a defective puppy. In most breeds this kind of problem is rare, but in a few breeds it is quite common. Again, by reading up on your breed you will know whether to expect any problems of this type.

One problem that can occur in any breed: the stomach has not completely closed up, and some of the intestines are on the outside. There is not much to do about this, and it is best to let the pup die. In order to save it, veterinary service is required to suture up the opening. Even if a veterinarian sutures the hole, you cannot be sure if any "parts" are missing. I have a friend who sutured up an opening himself. The pup died several days later, and the veterinarian commented: "You did just as well as I would have done."

Cleft palates are a very common problem in some breeds. A cleft palate and a hare lip will often occur together, and they are caused by failure of the bones of the palate to form completely. These puppies are unable to nurse and are put down at birth.

Edema—water puppies—is another common problem in some breeds. These are filled with fluid at the time of birth and are about twice the size of a normal whelp.

Doggie behavior belongs to the dogs! This adolescent Saint Bernard is teaching this very young pup about the canine bite — don't bite too hard!

They will die shortly after birth. Edema is common in only a few breeds—very uncommon in most breeds.

A mummified puppy turns up occasionally. A mummified pup is one whose development stopped during estrus; the fetus becomes a brownish lump or mass—sometimes recognized as a pup. Mummified pups can happen in any breed. In the breeders' survey I have listed the various descrip-tions of them. Of course, they are born dead and disposed of.

Do not waste time with defective pups. There are too many healthy pups being born who are looking for homes. Do not burden a pet owner with a defective pup. If you are breeding show dogs, do not burden *yourself* with these unfortunate pups. Keep the healthy, strong and viable pups; they will be the winners and the producers of the future.

Concentrate your attentions on the strong healthy puppies of the litter, these are the pups that will be the winners and companions of the future. This litter of Norwich Terrier pups were bred by Mrs. Johan Ostrow.

BREEDERS' SURVEY

Do you have many congenital defects in your breed? Obvious problems that are evident within minutes after birth?
Yes _4_ (Two Bulldog breeders and two Toy breeders)
No _22_
Do these puppies die or do you try to save them? Die
Have you had any mummified puppies? Yes _7_   No _19_
What do they look like?
Black, hard, underdeveloped mass; gray-brown matter and lumpy; dried up pup; seal-like and hairless.

The First Five Days

The Gaines Progress Report, Summer, 1980, opens its article titled "The Fading Syndrome, Septicemia and Other Puppy Diseases" with this observation: "It is estimated that 28% of all puppies die in the first week after birth." The first five days are the most critical days in a pup's life. Once through this period, a puppy's chances of survival are quite high. During this time, try to get everything going for the pups so as to enhance their chances of survival. The following guidelines should be carefully observed.

KEEP THE WHELPING BOX CLEAN

During the first two weeks mother will do most of the work for you, making the job easy. Change the bedding at least once a day—and twice if your mother has a lot of discharge. (C-sectioned mothers will have much more discharge than mothers of normally-whelped litters.)

CARE FOR THE MOTHER

Your daily chores for the first two weeks are really very few. They include checking over the pups, keeping the pen clean, and giving your bitch her normal care.

Make sure that the breast area of the mother is kept clean. In the summer months, do not allow her in areas where insecticides have been recently sprayed; and in the winter, keep her off sidewalks and driveways where salt has been spread. If you think there may be a problem with salt or insecticides, wash off her belly when you bring her inside.

Feed your mother two small meals a day rather than one large one. Give her some cottage cheese once a day. Be sure that she has access to water. It is easy for a mother to become dehydrated, particularly when the weather is hot.

CARE FOR THE PUPS

It is important that pups nurse soon after birth. The first milk contains colostrum, and this first milk provides immunity against diseases for the young pups. This colostrum provides passive immunity which can last up to sixteen weeks depending upon when the mother was last vaccinated. Dams vaccinated shortly before breeding will have the most immunity to pass along to pups. Those never vaccinated have little or no immunity to pass on. And some bitches may have some natural immunity to pass on.

Many pups have to have their toenails trimmed within the first few days following birth. Use a small pair of fingernail clippers and hold the pup in your hands. The nails contain little substance, and they can be trimmed quickly and readily, thus preventing pups from digging their nails into

It is important that the pups nurse soon after birth because the first milk contains colostrum which provides immunity against diseases. Breeder, Marcia Joslyn.

mother's breasts. As the puppies nurse, they knead the breasts to facilitate the milk flow, and long nails can leave many small bruises.

The umbilical cord will dry up and fall off in two to four days. Do not pull these off or worry about them; they take care of them-selves. You will eventually find them lying in the bottom of the box.

A few breeds will have to have dewclaws and/or tails docked by the third or fourth day. This will be a trying day for you and the mother, since the pups will be fussy and noisy. If one of the puppies is very small, the veteri-narian may wait on the tail dock until the seventh or eighth day. Be sure to know where the tail is to be docked on your particular breed, since not all veterinarians are knowledgeable about the requirements of individual breeds.

During this period you may find a dead pup in the pen in the morning. Mother and her off-spring may have seemed fine the night before, but now for no apparent reason a puppy has been pushed to the side of the pen and lies there dead. You might wish to take it to a veteri-narian for an autopsy. The veteri-narian will open the pup up and tell you if all of its organs are there—and if they are in the right place. Any further information will probably require that the pup be sent to a university veterinary school for a thorough autopsy. This will cost about the price of a nice dinner, and the results may take four to six weeks to reach you. It is best to accept the fact that the pup was not meant to be.

On the breeders' survey there was some disagreement about how much attention to give newborn pups. Some breeders sleep in the same room with the litters for the first night, and others stay up all night with them. Unless you have a breed that commonly has problems, you probably will not find it necessary to stay up nights with your pups. If you believe in the survival of the fittest (and these are the pups you want), a good, healthy pup will make it through the night without your assistance.

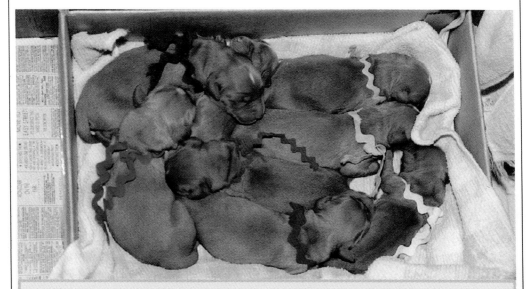

Note that each of these Golden Retriever puppies has his own color neckband so the breeder can determine one pup from another and monitor its growth.

BREEDERS' SURVEY

Do you ever find in necessary to stay up nights with your pups?
Of those who answered "yes," most stayed up only the first night.

Do you sleep in the same room with a newborn litter?
Yes __14__   No __13__ (My personal feeling is that bringing the litter into your bedroom requires a very tolerant sleeping partner.)

A quote on autopsies: "I have rarely autopsied puppies that died, but on several occasions when I was curious and did, I gained no knowledge about the cause of death. I feel it was a waste of time and money."

HEALTHY PUPS AND SICKLY PUPS

Feel your pups several times a day. Pick each one up in your hand, put your fingers around its body, and see how it feels to your hand. Put a puppy to your ear and listen to how it sounds.

A Healthy Pup:

1) Feels like a glove with a hand in it.
2) Sounds like a well-tuned motor.

A Sickly Pup:

1) Feels like a glove without a hand in it.
2) Sounds like it has emphysema.
3) Has a dull coat.
4) Is off in a corner of the box most of the time.
5) Nurses only for a few minutes and falls off—or does not nurse at all.
6) Has a tongue that is not as pink as you would like.
7) Feels cool.

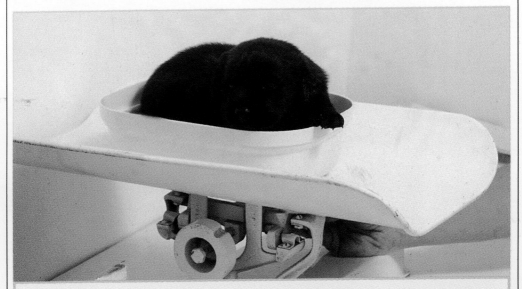

Steady weight gain indicates a healthy puppy and most breeders weigh their pups daily during their first week. This is a young Labrador pup owned by Emily Magnani.

3) Has a shiny coat.
4) Has a body that twitches when asleep.
5) Is strong enough to find the way to a nipple.
6) Nurses with conviction.
7) Has a pink tongue.
8) Feels warm.
9) Is quiet, either busy nursing or sleeping.
10) Has skin that pops back into place when "pinched."

8) Cries or sounds colicky.
9) Has skin that stays creased when "pinched."

WEIGHT GAIN

Weight gain is a good sign; it indicates a healthy puppy. Many of the breeders surveyed weigh their pups daily for the first week. Of those who don't, several said that they check their pups by "feel" and can tell when one does not feel right. Usually a pup that does not gain weight—and certainly one that loses weight—is in trouble. I used to weigh my pups daily, and I worried about those that were just maintaining their weight. Over the years I learned that a healthy pup is generally one that feels "good to the hand." Occasionally you will have a pup that just maintains its weight or gains very little—but feels healthy. This pup will probably do fine and will catch up to his littermates once it is on solid food. Most puppies will lose a bit of weight during the first twenty-four hours after birth, but by the second day they should start picking it up again.

TEMPERATURE

For the first twenty-four hours, the temperature of a pup is 94 degrees. Gradually it will climb to 95° and then to 97°. After three weeks the temperature should be 98° to 100°. The average temperature for an adult dog is between 101 and 102 degrees. Because of the initial low temperature, it is essential to keep the pups in a warm and draft-free environment. If the temperature of your pup is below 94 degrees, you have a serious problem. Remember when taking the temperature, put petroleum jelly on the bulb of the thermometer and insert it only for a minute or so.

It is essential to keep your pups in a draft-free and warm environment in order maintain their proper temperature. Golden Retriever litter nursing contentedly.

When the temperature drops, you are actually concerned with two problems. The first is the drop in temperature. The second is the *cause*: why did it drop in the first place? If you do get the pup warmed up, you still have not dealt with the basic problem that caused the temperature to drop. There is no reason to believe that the problem was solved by the warming of the puppy.

DEHYDRATION

Dehydration occurs when an insufficient amount of fluid gets into the system. Test for dehydration by pinching the skin on the back or neck. If the skin stays creased in place after the pinch, the puppy is dehydrated. Sometimes in a slow starting pup the problem will correct itself once the pup begins nursing well. Other times dehydration is a sign of a sickly pup.

Danger Signs for Pups: temperature drop, no weight gain, dehydration.

WHAT CAUSES SICKLY PUPS?

1) Drafts or unhealthy whelping conditions.

2) Toxic milk.

3) A genetic problem.

4) An internal problem.

5) Fading puppy syndrome. This occurs when an apparently healthy pup fails to gain weight, quits nursing and fades away. The cause for this condition is unknown, but it is thought by some veterinarians to be caused by a virus.

6) Respiratory problem. The pup cannot breathe right and it cannot nurse. Numbers 4, 5 and 7 can all be put in this category.

7) Mother sat on puppy and it could no longer breathe. (I had one of these. Good grief! It looked like a pancake!)

THE CURSE OF A SICKLY PUP

A sickly pup takes all of your time. Each time you look in the box your eye and hand travel to the sickly one, while you let mother take care of the healthy ones. Sickly pups take a tremendous amount of time. They tap your emotions and, in general, sap your energies and reserves.

THE JOY OF A HEALTHY PUP

A healthy pup is a viable, living being, and you don't have to worry about it. Mother takes care of the pup and its needs, and the pup just keeps growing and looking better each day.

BREEDERS' SURVEY

How often do you weigh your pups?

Most of those who weigh the pups daily do so for the first week only and then weigh weekly after that.

One comment: "I hold them each day and know if all is well."

Treating Sickly Pups

In order to identify a sickly pup, watch for a pup that spends a lot of time in a corner of the pen by himself. This pup has apparently made no effort to get to mother, and she has not tried to bring the pup to her. Keep an eye on this pup. Weigh it daily and feel it to see if it seems plump and warm. Something is usually wrong with a puppy that is off by itself all of the time.

If you have a litter of only one puppy—and that pup is not healthy—you can be deceived. You have nothing to compare it to. As a pup gets older, its fur grows; so a single pup can look bigger—and healthier—then it actually is. It may not be growing at all. I do weigh single puppies more often just to make sure that they are progressing. Once a pup starts going downhill, it slides very quickly. Most "sickies" last less than thirty-six hours; however, it can seem like *days* to you.

At times one pup in the litter does not seem as perky as the rest, although it does not appear to be really sickly. The pup may be smaller than the others and may be a little dehydrated. Be sure that this pup is getting on a nipple as often as the big pups. You can remove all the other pups but the small one and let him nurse for awhile by himself. Sometimes if you supplement-feed this pup twice a day or so, you can get him up to his littermates within a week.

Sickly and dead pups are all a part of puppy rearing. Like it or not, sickness and death are actually nature's way of culling a litter. Not all pups are meant to live. Often times your mother will have more sense than you. Her instinct will tell her when there is something wrong with a pup, and she will push it out of the way and completely disregard its cries. Breeders who live on farms have more common sense about the "survival of the fittest" theory. A friend who has raised both cattle and pigs told me years ago that she never tries to save a puppy that has been pushed aside by its mother. She knows that both nature and the bitch are telling her something.

HANDLING THE SICKLY PUP
Take the pup out of the box and examine it. Put it to your ear and listen. If you hear a wheezing sound, the pup probably has a respiratory problem. If the pup cannot breathe, he cannot nurse; and if he cannot nurse, he cannot survive. When babies have respiratory problems, they are put on a respirator. You cannot do this with puppies.

Is there a discharge around the mouth? Clean it up with a tissue. Any bloody discharge around the anus? Check the color in case you want to report this to the veteri-

narian. Check the nostrils. Sometimes they will almost be sealed
shut with a discharge and will
need to be cleaned out. This
procedure can be tricky; you are
handling something that weighs
only a few ounces, and cotton
swabs are usually too big for the
job. Use a toothpick instead. Hold
the pup in a strong light and
carefully clean out the nostrils. If
you want to see if the pup is
breathing through its nose, hold a
hair in front of the nose and see if
the hair moves.

Sick pups need to get warmed
up—but warmed up gradually.
You can warm a pup by putting
him under your sweater next to
your skin or by putting him in
the ready box with a hot water
bottle. During this process do
not feed the puppy. As the pup
cools down, his digestive system
starts to shut off. If you feel the
pup has warmed up, mix a
teaspoon of honey (sugar or corn
syrup will do if you do not have
honey on hand) with an ounce of
very hot water. Mix this until it

is dissolved. By the time you
have done this, the temperature
of the water will have dropped
enough to give him a chance to
swallow. If it stays down, repeat
every half hour for several
hours. Sometimes this simple
syrup mixture works very
effectively in perking up a slow
pup. If your simple syrup
mixture continues to stay down
and if your pup warms up and
appears to be doing well, begin
either hand feeding the pup or
allowing him to nurse.

In my younger years, I spent
many hours (and tears) trying to
save sick puppies. I have yet to
save one that eventually
amounted to anything. Consequently, I spend a lot less time
with them now. Your pup may
pull through the first day, and
you may feel that you have pulled
off a major accomplishment (and
you have). Invariably, however,
this pup dies the second or third
day. In most cases these life
saving measures only prolong life.
The biggest problem is that you

BREEDERS' SURVEY

Do you make any superhuman efforts to save a puppy that obviously looks like it is leaving the world? Yes **10**   No **13**
Comments: "Yes, I made a superhuman effort and they all died."
"Yes, and regretted it later."
"I have not had the problems, but I would not do so."
"No, not any more."
"I generally don't bother much with a weak, sickly puppy. I feel that this is nature's way, and if it lives, fine; if not, also fine. I don't care to have a weak, sickly dogs about and run up a bunch of vet bills for inferior type stock."
And a last, plaintive cry: "Yes, it kills me to lose one."

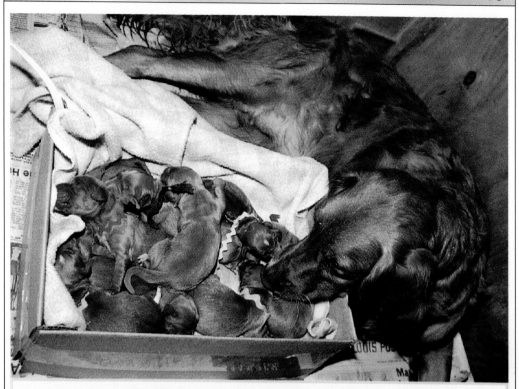

This is Chances R' Chaser watching over her litter. Breeder, Nona Kilgore Bauer.

do not know what is wrong with the puppy. Is he missing something internally? Does he have a virus? An ex-ray won't tell you anything because the pup is much too small.

Even though these sickly pups usually die, it does seem that a person should take some measures to try and pull them through. Should you make a superhuman effort? See the breeders' survey for some interesting comments.

DEATH IS COMING

Once a pup begins cooling down, it usually dies in six to thirty-six hours. This is not a pleasant subject, but it must be discussed: it is a fact of puppy-rearing.

You can do one of two things if you think the pup is beyond your help and is dying:

1) You can take the pup to the veterinarian, and he will fill it with Ringer's solution. This puffs the pup up and makes him feel good to the hand. The veterinarian will give the pup a couple of shots, charge you the price of a good dinner and tell you to call him in the A.M. Most of the time this pup will be dead in the A.M. If it is not, consider it a miracle and call the veterinarian. (Back in the days when I did this, I never had a pup live long enough to go back for a second visit.)

2) You can put a warm hot water bottle in your ready box together with some fluffy towels—and your pup. Cover

him up and leave him alone. Again, this pup will usually be dead in the A.M. However, I feel that this pup has at least gone onward with a little dignity. If you leave this pup with the mother, she will push it off to the side, causing it to be cold and unhappy. It will cry and look terribly pathetic. (Mother often appears as though she can't hear or see a thing, and that makes the event twice as sad.) When placed in the ready box, the pup stays in one place, remains warm and usually cries a lot less.

Neither situation is ideal, but death never is. It is always depressing to lose a pup regardless of how many years you have been breeding dogs. However, it does seem easier to lose one at three or four days—or to have one born dead—than to lose one at two or three months. You must realize that the more litters you have, the more dead pups you will handle. Each individual will develop his own psychology for coping with the death of a puppy. In time you will find yours.

The method for disposing of dead pups is up to you. I buried one pup—an eight-week girl that was hard to lose. We wrapped her in a towel, placed her in a shoe box and then in a plastic bag, and buried her. Where else but in the rose garden? This was just as the first parvovirus problem had developed. Several hours later I received a call from my veterinarian who said that the university would probably want to do an autopsy on the body. "Gee, do you think I should dig it up?" "Yes." So I dug that box up, put it in another plastic bag, and put it in the freezer of a restaurant that we owned. I worried for *days* that the health inspector would come by before the university did.

Putting dead pups in the freezer is common practice for breeders who want to have them checked out by a university at a later date. Do remember that they are there: it is embarrassing to have them drop out when non-dog company is present. This happened to a friend while guests were sitting around waiting for a drink. My eyes got large as I saw this plastic bag bounce out of the freezer onto the floor. My friend's eyes got even larger as he put his head behind the freezer door and mouthed, "dead puppy!"

An old adage says "A cold puppy is a dead puppy." Keep this in mind as you handle your puppies. Sickly pups are time consuming, emotionally draining and unrewarding. A sickly pup will die most of the time no matter what is done. The survivors will oftentimes be mediocre at best—and often sickly as adults.

Sometimes outside influences play a part in your efforts to keep a pup going. If you have a litter of six and the only female starts turning cold, you will want to make a bigger effort to save her. If it is a litter of one, you will want to try harder. And if you have a lot of money invested in the litter—stud fee, shipping costs and perhaps Cesarean section expenses—you will want to try even harder to save a puppy.

Possible Problems for a Nursing Bitch

The following problems can occur with a nursing bitch:
- Caked Breasts (Galactostasis)
- Mastitis
- Toxic milk
- Eclampsia (milk fever)
- Failure to accept pups

CAKED BREASTS (GALACTOSTASIS)

Caked breasts occur when the bitch produces more milk than is being used. This condition can be more prevalent with a litter of one or two pups than with a litter of six or eight. Check the bitch's breasts daily, especially the two rear ones, as this is where the problem will usually start. Breasts that are caked up will be swollen (or feel hard) along the milk glands. If this condition is left alone, the breast will simply dry up. But, occasionally, caked breasts can lead to other problems such as mastitis. Some veterinarians think that you should leave

There are many problems that can occur with a nursing bitch: each problem has certain negative effects on the health of the mother and her litter. Labrador litter owned by Diane Ammerman.

these breasts alone. They will either dry up within three to five days or your pups will start nursing on them and they will gradually return to normal. Most breeders like to hand nurse these breasts down if for no other reason than to relieve the bitch of her discomfort. I find that my pups do not nurse on these big, hard breasts; so I cannot count on the pups for any help. When I get the breasts down to normal size, the pups start nursing on them again and the problem is alleviated.

To nurse the breasts down, make a hot pack with a washcloth and lay it on the infected breasts for a few minutes. Then, milk these breasts down *only* to the point that tightness eases. The more you milk the breasts, the more milk that is produced; therefore, you do not want to nurse them dry, as the problem will just continue. Nurse them down two or three times a day within a few days and they will return to normal.

MASTITIS

Mastitis is a bacterial infection of the mammary glands, and it is a problem that needs immediate veterinary attention because the infection can turn into an abscess. The breasts turn red to purple and the bitch becomes listless, dehydrated and fevered. Usually only one or two breasts become involved. These one or two nipples can be taped, and the puppies can usually continue to be raised on the other breasts.

TOXIC MILK

Toxic milk is a condition that is attributed to incompatibility of puppies to the bitch's milk. Watch for a litter that is not gaining weight and be particularly concerned if the puppies start to persistently cry and sound colicky. Quite often their rectums will become red and swollen and their stools runny. Take your bitch and the puppies to the veterinarian and have them checked over. Failure to take care of this problem can lead to the death of the complete litter. If the mother does have toxic milk, the puppies will have to be raised by hand.

ECLAMPSIA (MILK FEVER)

Eclampsia is not an uncommon problem. It is caused by an upset in the calcium regulatory mechanism. The first signs are restlessness and anxiety in the bitch. She will pace up and down with a stiff-legged gait, and it will not be uncommon for her to fall over. Her temperature may get as high as 106 degrees. Take your bitch to the veterinarian immediately if she starts showing these symptoms. He will give her calcium intravenously, and she should return to normal shortly. Pups may be taken off the dam for a few hours, but they are usually able to resume nursing. In very severe cases, the pups may have to be removed from the mother permanently. If the pups are close to three weeks old when removed, start to wean them.

You can be assured that all is going well with nursing if both the mother and the litter seem content and satisfied. Breeder, Virginia Matanic.

WHAT YOU WANT TO SEE WHEN YOU LOOK AT MOTHER AND PUPS

When you look in the whelping box or pen, you want to see a content mother—and a contented litter.

Your mother should be eating well, drinking water and giving off an air of well-being. The puppies should be tucked up around her, alternately sleeping or nursing. They should be quiet, happy and warm.

On rare occasions your bitch will not produce enough milk to feed the litter. Your pups will be crying because they are hungry, and your bitch's breasts will be small and will look empty. If you nurse one of these breasts, you will see that the milk flow is poor. If it is, take your bitch to the veterinarian for a shot that will let the milk down.

If mother is eating poorly or refusing food completely or showing any signs of distress such as vomiting, fever or listlessness, you have a problem. If your puppies are not nursing, are not gaining weight and are crying continually, you also have a problem. If any of these symptoms develop, take your pups and the bitch to the veterinarian without delay and have them checked over. Something is wrong.

FAILURE TO ACCEPT PUPS

Occasionally—but rarely—a mother will refuse to accept her pups. If this occurs put the pups with the bitch for nursing five or six times a day. You will have to hold her head down, and you may have to hold her in place. You will also have to clean the pups. Before giving the pups to the mother to nurse, show the mother

Sometimes a mother will show disinterest and refuse to feed her pups, but she usually will come around in time. These puppies seem to have no problems!

a pup (show her the rump, not the head) and let her sniff it. Squeeze some milk from her breasts onto the pup and see if she licks it. You might also rub a little liver on the pup to attract her interest. Once the mother starts to lick the pup, her interest should become awakened. Watch the mother very closely if you think that she may snap. Very often these bitches come around to an accepting mood in three or four days; but until they do, they take *a lot* of patience. (At this point, you will *really* wonder why it was so important to have this litter.) If your bitch starts crying for her pups, your battle is won and she is ready for them. Sometimes these mothers turn out to

be good mothers; they're just terribly slow starters. This unwillingness to mother pups is similar, but not the same, as the unwillingness that Cesarean sectioned mothers display.

HOW TO SEPARATE THE BITCH FROM HER PUPS

Always keep your pups on the mother if at all possible. However, if your veterinarian has determined that the puppies must be taken off the bitch, for whatever reason, you should first separate the bitch and pups physically as much as possible. The less she hears the puppies, the easier it will be on her—and you. This will be a trying time for you and the bitch.

Unless there is a specific problem, keep your pups with their mother as much as possible.

The breasts dry up within a week if you do nothing with them; and this is the course of action that many veterinarians recommend. Again, many breeders like to nurse the breasts down a bit to at least relieve some of the tightness and to help the bitch become more comfortable. Some breeders advising rubbing oil of camphor on the breasts while milking them down in order to dry them up more quickly.

Regardless of whether you milk them down, use oil of camphor or just let the breasts dry up naturally, you should cut the mother's food intake by one-third. The more she eats, the more nutrition she gets and the more milk she produces. Once the breasts are just about dried up, you can increase her food intake back to normal.

A bitch who is separated from her pups will be continually unhappy for close to a week. However, if separation is required, you have no choice but to forge ahead.

ORPHAN PUPPIES

Toxic milk, severe eclampsia, mastitis, failure to accept pups and the death of the mother are conditions that create orphan pups. Raising orphan pups is a challenge—but one that can be dealt with. The biggest problem is the amount of time that it takes. Make every effort to keep the pups with the mother. Hand-

If there is some reason your bitch cannot nurse, you must find other ways to feed your pups. Bottle feeding is one way to nourish puppies that are not able to nurse. This Pug baby was bred by Anna Benedetto.

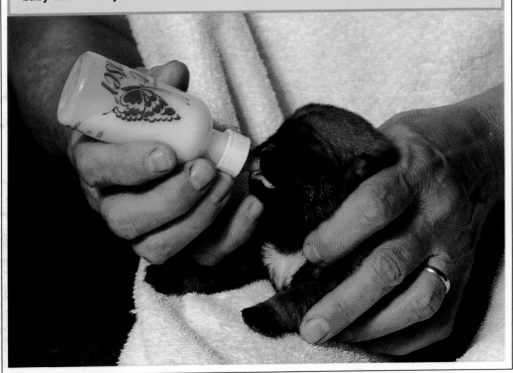

raising is a poor substitute for the job that mother can do. If possible, locate a foster mother who can take the pups. This sounds easier than it actually is. You must find a nursing bitch, one with pups that are less than four weeks old. If this bitch already has six pups or so, her owner is probably not going to be thrilled at the prospect of more puppies. Try to find an experienced dam who is owned by a kindly, old-time breeder. Preferably the foster mother should be raising only two or three pups. The foster mother's breed does not make any difference. I had one litter of Scottish Terriers raised on a Chihuahua and one litter raised by a Pug. I have also heard of cats raising litters of puppies.

The first step in raising pups on a foster mother is to put your pups in the ready box with a hot water bottle and take them to the foster mother. All the pups should be healthy; it is not fair to give sickly pups to a new mother. Let the *owner of the foster mother* handle your pups and her bitch. The owner of the bitch should first let the mother carefully sniff one of the new pups. Then, she should rub one of the "old" pups over one of the "new" ones. If the old pup urinates on the new pup, hand the new pup to the mother and see if she will clean it. If she does, or if she shows any interest in the new pup, attach the new pup to a good, working nipple and see if the pup begins to suck. A "good, working" nipple is one that a strong puppy is already nursing

on vigorously. This nipple is "ready to go;" simply pull off the old pup and put on the new one. A strong new pup will quickly take over, and the old pup will find a new nipple. Once a new pup is accepted, go on to the next new pup. Again, let the owner of the bitch do all of this. If she is working with a good mother, the mother will quickly accept these pups and you can leave. Occasionally a young mother may be a bit slow in accepting new pups. And pups that have been tubed (hand-fed) for four or five days may need to be taught how to nurse. If so, open the pup's mouth with your finger, hold him up to a nipple, and put the nipple into his mouth. After a few tries the pup will take hold and begin to suck.

When it is time to pick up your pups, bring along a small gift—or perhaps some money—for the owner of the foster mother. If you give money, the amount is up to you.

Raising pups that have been orphaned can be a challenge, but it is possible to raise healthy puppies by hand. These Dalmatian puppies are well fed and sleeping happily. Breeder, Margaret Keenan.

Raising Pups by Hand

Three factors must be considered in hand-raising a litter:
1) Warmth
2) Nourishment
3) Sanitation

KEEPING THE PUPS WARM

Keep the pups in your whelping pen if you are using a pen. Otherwise keep them in a wire crate or a cardboard box. You must get these pups off the floor. This keeps them out of the drafts, and it also will save your back, since you will be doing a lot of bending over the box. Let's assume that you have chosen to use a wire crate. Put the crate on a table (a dining room table, for instance) and wrap a sheet around all four sides of the crate, using clamp clothespins to hold the sheet in place. Clamp your reflector lamp on the side of the crate. Put some newspapers in the bottom of the crate and place a towel on top of the newspapers. Fill one or two hot water bottles with hot water. Fill them half-full so that they resemble a water bed. Wrap each bottle in a towel and place one at each end of the crate. Put an old sweater at one end of the crate. This same arrangement can be used in a whelping pen, although you may want to make the area smaller by placing boxes or other barriers in the pen.

Your pups should now stay warm. It is more difficult to keep a single puppy warm than a litter, as several pups together can provide each other warmth. The old, fluffy sweater can really serve as a good substitute mother for the loner.

Nourishment

On the breeders' survey, twenty-three breeders used some kind of commercial formula that can be obtained from your veterinarian. This formula is a substitute for mother's milk. It is always a good idea to have a can of formula on hand when you are expecting puppies.

You can get the formula into your pups in one of the three ways: by eyedropper, by baby bottle, or by stomach tube.

Eyedropper

Feeding by eyedropper is only a stop-gap remedy until you can get your equipment set up. You may have to make a quick trip to the veterinarian for formula, syringe, or other equipment. (Pups can go for a few hours without feeding; when they are hungry they will start to cry.) When using an eyedropper, fill it about half-full of formula and slowly squeeze it into the pup's mouth. As a feeding method, this is tedious, time consuming and relatively ineffective.

Baby Bottle or Doll's Bottle

If you use a bottle, you will usually have to enlarge the holes in the nipple with a sewing

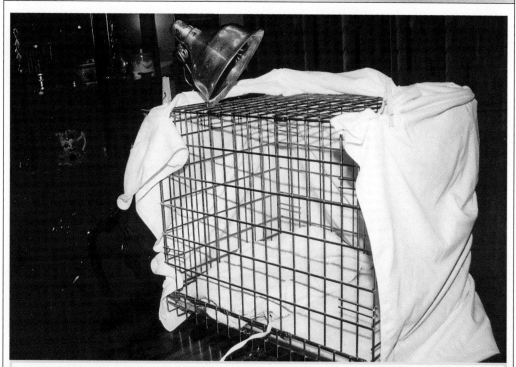

An orphan puppy box during the day, with adequate room, heat and ventilation.

An orphan puppy box at night.

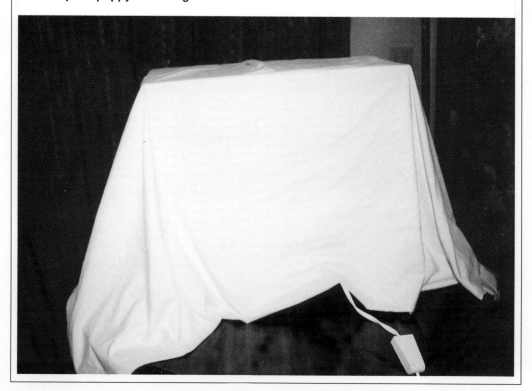

needle. Many of the breeders said they used both a baby bottle and the tubing method for hand-feeding. Bottle feeding is time consuming; and with bottles you do not know exactly how much formula the pup is getting.

Warm your formula to room temperature before feeding. Formula can be quickly warmed by filling a metal food pan half-way with hot tap water and, after estimating about how much formula you will need, putting it in a china cup or dish and setting it in the pan. Stir the formula a little, and within two or three minutes it will warm to room temperature. When you open your formula put it into two clean, glass containers. You will work from one container, and you will store the other container in the refrigerator until you need it. This way at least half of your formula will not be constantly opened and exposed. The shelf life for formula seems to be about three weeks. It should smell sweet and be of good color. When old, it starts to ferment. The proportion of formula fed for bottle-fed puppies is the same as for tube-fed puppies.

I know many breeders who bottle-feed with success. I have tried all kinds of bottles, with different-sized holes in the nipples, and I have always felt that I could never live long enough to bottle-feed a litter. It's too time consuming. Obviously it is helpful to have young children around who are trained to do this.

When hand feeding a pup, make sure to warm the formula and chart the amount and time of each feeding.

Tube Feeding (Gavage Method)

Tube feeding is really an easy, quick (about two minutes per pup), accurate method of feeding. Tube feeding requires two pieces of equipment, which you can obtain from your veterinarian. You need a soft catheter (your veterinarian will know the size for your pups) and a plastic syringe. Don't think that you will kill the pup by tube feeding it; this is hard to do (but not impossible). I learned how to tube feed over the telephone from a Boston Terrier breeder. (My first phone call was to a Great Dane breeder: "Take a syringe the size of a turkey baster and fill it with 80 cc of formula." 80 cc! I didn't know much in those days, but I knew that I could feed a litter of six for a week on that!)

If hand-feeding, you *must* have a scale to weigh your pups, since the amount that is fed is based

DAILY HAND FEEDING CHART

Puppy	Weight	Amt. Fed	Times Fed
1 Male, Black	10 oz.	10 cc	8 a.m, 2 p.m, 8 p.m, 12 a.m.
2 Female, Black	9 oz.	9 cc	"
3 Male, Brindle	9 oz.	9 cc	"
4 Female, Brindle	5 oz.	6 cc	"
5 Male, Red	8 oz.	8 cc	"

WEEKLY HAND FEEDING RECORDS

Puppy #	Day and Weight						
	1	2	3	4	5	6	7
1	10 oz.	10½ oz	11 oz	12 oz	13½ oz	14 oz.	15 oz
2	9	9	11	12½	13	14	14
3	9	10	11	12	12	13	13½
4	5	6	7	8	9	10	10
5	8	8	9½	10	10	11½	13

Hand feeding chart.

upon the weight of each pup. The feeding formula that most breeders like for either bottle-fed or tubed puppies is this: *one cc for each ounce of body weight four times a day.* Therefore, if you have a ten-ounce pup, you will give it 10 cc of formula four times a day—10 cc each feeding time—for a total of 40 cc a day.

If you are either bottle feeding or tube feeding, you must keep a running record of the time of day that the pups were fed and the amount that they were fed. Unless you write it down, it is very easy to forget when and how much you have fed.

If you follow the above feeding formula, the pup's stool should be normal. If you are overfeeding, the stools will be a greenish color. If so, cut back a bit on the amount of formula. If the puppy appears healthy but cries often, it probably is hungry and should be fed a little more. If this happens, increase the amount of formula gradually or give it a smaller fifth feeding. If the puppy appears healthy and contented but a little dehydrated (remember how to pinch the skin to check for dehydration?), give him four ccs or so of water several times a day between feeding of the formula.

If you do not have any commercial formula on hand and you are unable to get any for a day or so, the following formulas can be used: 1 cup whole milk, 1 egg yolk. Blend together. Or 1-13 oz can evaporated milk, 3 oz of water, 1 tbs. of corn syrup. Blend together.

Note that young pups cannot digest egg whites. If you add eggs to their food, give them the yolks only.

To begin the tube feeding, first measure outside the pup with the catheter the distance from the pup's mouth to the stomach, which is located at the level of the last rib. Mark the distance on the tube with a piece of tape. As your pups grow you will have to move the marker; and if your pups are of different sizes, you will have to have more than one marker on your tube. You are now ready.

Before tube feeding, first measure outside the pup with the catheter the distance from the pup's mouth to his stomach.

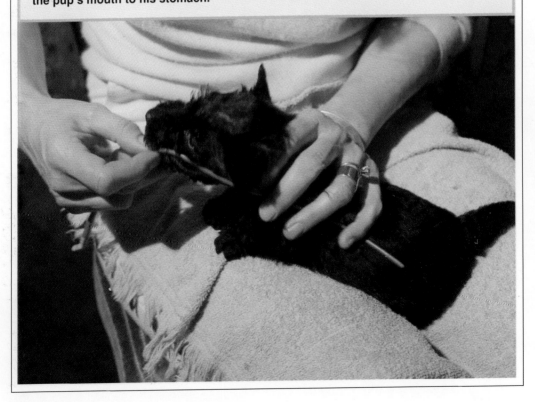

1) Fill your syringe with the proper amount of room temperature formula.

2) Put the "flap" on the "tube" (catheter).

3) Put this equipment in a dish—or on some paper—and place on a table.

4) Sit in a chair next to the table with the towel in your lap.

5) Put the pup on your lap, stomach down, front legs on your right leg and rear legs between your legs.

6) Gently thread the tube down the pup's mouth. (After several days, your pup will swallow the tube on its own.) *Do not push.* If the pup gags, withdraw the tube and start over. Use a steady pressure and thread the tube down to the tape marker. If you meet an obstacle, pull the tube out and start over. *Do not jam the tube down the throat.* If the tube seems to stick, put a little formula around the tip of the tube to help it go down easier.

7) Put your left hand over the pup's head and hold the tube *and* the head with your left hand. With your right hand undo the flap on the tube and attach the filled syringe. (Some veterinarians will give you a tube that does not have the flap. If this happens, attach the syringe directly to the tube. This gives you a little more to hold in your hand.

8) Slowly push in the plunger on the syringe until all the formula is gone. Your pup may squeak a bit, and as he gets older and stronger he will struggle. Just hold firmly on to the head and the tube, and all of the formula will go where it is supposed to go.

9) With your right hand (while still holding on to the head and tube with your left hand) remove the syringe, attach the flap and remove the tube.

All this may sound complicated and time consuming—but it really isn't. You can take care of each pup's feeding in two minutes time, from start to finish. It will take another minute to clean each pup. You can tube and clean a litter of five (from the time you get out your formula until you clean everything up) in twenty minutes. Do not let old wives' tales scare you. Tube-feeding is easy and it is *much* quicker and more accurate than bottle feeding. It is the best way to feed.

Advantages of tube feeding:

1) You can feed more quickly by tube than by bottle.

2) You know the exact amount of formula each puppy gets.

3) You have to feed only four times a day, once every six hours. This means that you can get a night's sleep or go to a party without being interrupted after two hours.

Some notes:

1) The flap prevents formula from spilling out on the way to the stomach.

2) Many tubed pups died because it is common to tube sickly pups or pups that are not nursing, hoping to improve them. A sickly pup will probably die whether or not he is tubed. Do not feed formula to pups that are

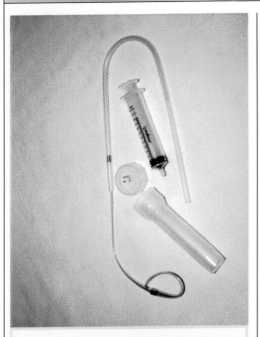

Tube feeding equipment: a soft catheter and a plastic syringe.

cold, since they are unable to digest it.

3) You have nothing to lose by tubing. If you do not tube or bottle-feed an orphan litter, it will die from lack of nourishment.

4) If, by chance, the tube gets into the lungs, your pup will die pronto, as you have essentially drowned him. Therefore, if you are tubing a sickly pup and he dies two hours later, don't think you have killed him. If you thread your tube down carefully and gently all the way to the marker, you should not have any problems. I have not talked to any breeders who have drowned a puppy by tubing.

5) Some veterinarians will suggest that you feed more than

Tube feeding a puppy.

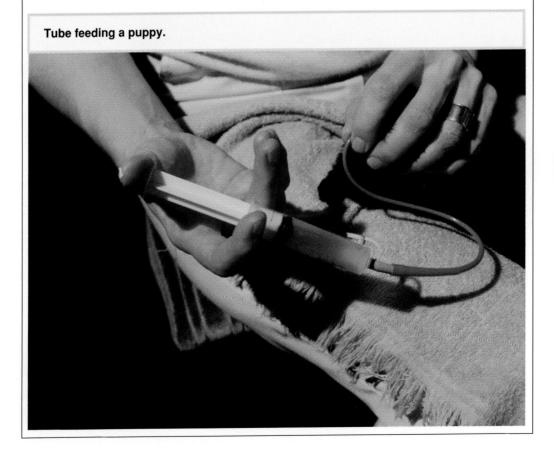

four times a day (five or six times) and give less formula each time. If you do, the total amount of formula given for a day will remain the same as if you fed four times a day.

6) Be sure to wash your equipment when you are through using it. The formula is sticky, and it will be difficult to get it out of the tube if you let it sit for very long. If this should happen, soak the tube in a pan of hot water.

CLEANING THE ORPHAN PUP

When a litter is raised by its mother, the pups' reflexes are stimulated through her licking, and, consequently, the pups urinate and defecate. When a mother is not around, you have to clean the pups yourself. After you have tubed each pup, take a tissue and rub from the fanny to the stomach on the male pups and from the stomach to the tail on the female pups, and they will immediately urinate. Put a dab of baby oil on a cotton ball and rub around the anus. The pup will usually defecate. Two stools a day are sufficient for a pup. If a pup goes for thirty-six hours without defecating, call your veterinarian to find out if you should be concerned.

As you tube and clean each pup, it is a good idea to put the tubed ones into the ready box so that you can keep the fed and unfed pups separate. Unless you are working with only two pups, or if they are all marked differently, it is very easy to forget which you have fed and which you have not. Of course, they won't tell you!

After each feeding, check the puppy box and clean if necessary. (Contrary to the books, hand-raised pups will pop out a poop on their own.) Refill your hot water bottle and put your pups back into their crate or box.

This is the formula for hand-raising pups. It takes time. But you can hold a regular job and still do it, provided that you or someone can get home at noon to feed. I have a male friend who hand-raised a litter of eight Brittanys while working. If he could do it so can you!

BREEDERS' SURVEY

If it is necessary to supplement feed, do you tube feed? **18**
Do you bottle feed? **13**

Seven breeders said they have both tube fed and bottle fed. Two breeders used both a commercial formula *and* their own formula. Three breeders never had to supplement feed, but all the other breeders have. Some breeders think that tubed pups lack a sucking reflex, and for that reason they like to bottle feed as well as tube feed. Tubed pups may suck on one another's genitalia. But normally raised pups will do that, too.

IMPORTANT TIPS

1) Push your pups around a bit with your finger. Give them some attention in addition to the feeding. They don't have a mother around to attend to them.

2) Hand-raising pups is a messy business in case you haven't already figured this out. Your dining room table, or whatever table you use, probably has a crate sitting on it, a ready box to hold just-fed pups, a pile of clean towels, cotton balls, tissue box, pad and paper. The kitchen counter always seems to have some formula stuck to it. Accept it and learn to live with it. You have no choice anyway.

3) Hand-raised pups do not grow at the same rate as mother-reared pups. *Do not worry* if your pups do little more than hold their weight for four or five days. You are really using the scale to determine how much formula you should be giving them, not to see how much they are gaining every day. As long as the pups "feel" good and are not crying you have no problems.

4) Hand-raised pups generally look "tacky." They do not have very healthy or shiny coats, and, of course, they are small. By three to four months they will catch up to a mother-raised litter.

5) Hand-raised pups can start very early on food. Actually, all

This is one of a litter of ten bottle-fed Doberman puppies. Breeders, Chris and Dara Swendsen.

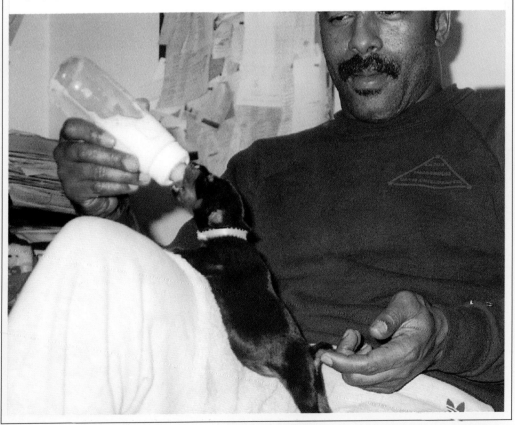

Hand-raised puppies usually have great dispositions due to the individual attention and caring they have received from their breeder. Cocker litter bred by Ellen Passage.

pups can start on solid food at an early age, but you do not have to hurry a pup when a mother is available for nursing. *As soon as your pup's eyes are open and he can stand, introduce food to him.* Use the same solid food formulas as you would use on mother-reared dogs, but make it more of a gruel, since your puppies still do not have any teeth. Dilute the food with both formula and water and make it very mushy. For at least a week or so, you will have to tube feed in addition to feeding solid food—but use your judgment on this. If you have a good eater—and many hand-raised pups are hearty eaters—you can probably stop tubing sooner. Once pups get on solids, they start to gain weight quickly, which is all the more reason to get them on solids early.

After the pups are on their way, move them out of their crate or box into a larger area such as the whelping pen. Notice that you will have gradually stopped cleaning them—as they now do this job by themselves.

I like to give hand-raised pups a good liquid vitamin that contains liver, but this is the only supplement that I use. Vitamins can be obtained from your veterinarian. Be sure to keep water available for the pups when you start them on solids.

Again, remember:

1) Hand-raise a litter only as a last resort. It is better to hand-raise than to have the litter die.

2) Hand-raised pups are slow in developing during the first six weeks.

3) Raising a litter by hand is time consuming.

4) Hand-raised pups can have terrific dispositions, especially if a pup is the only one in the litter. They have received a lot of individual attention because you, in essence, have been their mother!

5) A hand-raised pup or litter is personally rewarding.

GOOD LUCK!

Your Puppies Are Growing

Sometimes between the ages of ten and eighteen days your puppies' eyes will open. They will look like deep blue orbs, and they will not focus. It will take two to three weeks after the eyes open before they are able to track a rolling ball—and before they acquire their adult eye color. Observe the eyes as they start to open. First, a crack will form in the corner of the eye, and then over a period of several days they will gradually open all the way. Do not force the eyes to open. Let them open on their own. Occasionally a "pus pocket" forms under the eyelid causing the eyelid to bulge. When this happens, hold a warm washcloth on the eye for a few minutes and carefully apply a little pressure to the corner of the eye with your finger. The "goo" will come out of the slit of the opening and should be wiped off. Check the eye several times a day to see if goo is building up again. Pus pockets present no serious problem and do not require any veterinary care. Once the eye opens up completely, the problem goes away. At the time the eyes open, the ears will start to open up. At around three weeks the pups can usually hear loud noises such as the bark of a nearby adult dog.

At around two weeks, your puppies will be standing, and by three weeks they will be walking. The longer the pup's leg, the earlier he will get up. Short-legged breeds can be slower to begin moving about, and they often move backwards first. By four weeks, the pups should be up on their legs, walking (perhaps wobbly), seeing large objects, and hearing fairly well. They should also be more aware of each other and should start playing together. Remember to continue to trim the toenails.

WEANING

Breeders wean pups anytime between two and one-half weeks and five weeks. Hand-raised pups should be started on solid food as early as possible—as soon as their eyes open and they can stand. I like to introduce food to my pups at an early age. All puppies are interested in solids anytime between three and four weeks, and many are interested earlier than that. When pups start nosing around mother's dish, it is a sure sign that they are getting ready to

Puppies can be weaned and started on solid foods at an early age, from anywhere between two-and-a-half and five weeks of age. These young Cockers were bred by Patty Darke.

eat solid food. Offer the pups a bit of her food on your finger. If they lick it, start giving them some solid food of their own.

Start your pups on a good brand name of puppy chow or kibble, preferably the same brand you feed your adults. Soak the kibble or chow in water until it becomes soft. This may take several hours for some brands and a half-hour for others. Some breeders run the food through their food processor or blender, but this procedure is not necessary if you let it soak long enough. For small breeds, start with approximately half a cup of dry kibble or chow and cover with water. When this is thoroughly softened, add about a teaspoon of an all-meat dog food or baby beef, which serves as an added incentive for the pups to start eating. I then add a teaspoon of baby egg yolk and mix thoroughly, mashing any lumps with a fork. If you hand-raised and have any formula left over, add about a tablespoon of formula and then add enough water to make a thin gruel. At this point, your pups barely have teeth and will not be able to chew well. If you wish, put some cottage cheese in the food once a day. The main basis of the meal, though, *must* be some form of dog chow or kibble. Do not feed your pups canned meat.

The breeders' survey indicates that many breeders start out with hamburger and rice cereal. Each time you change a pup's food, you take a chance of upsetting the intestinal tract. Therefore, if you go from mother's milk to baby

Start your puppies out on a good brand name of puppy chow or kibble, mixed with dog food and egg yolk, and softened to a gruel-like consistency. Breeders, Ed and Glenna Carlson.

cereal to puppy chow to adult chow, you change food four times. By skipping the baby cereal, you have one less chance for problems. And most pups readily take to the puppy chow. (In addition, puppies *really* get sticky on baby cereal.) Wash and keep your baby food jars such as those the egg yolks come in. They are handy containers for stool samples.

When you feed the pups the first time, put all the puppies in the corner of the whelping box and push the food pan up to them. The earlier you start to feed, the greater tendency for some of the pups to back away from the pan. By placing them in the corner, they have nowhere to go. Run your fingers through the food and offer it to each puppy. Usually the females start to eat several days before the males. For the slow ones, dab some food on

When feeding, use large straight-sided pans to ensure each puppy gets his fill and no food is spilled or wasted.

their feet or legs; they will lick it off and get the idea that the gruel is good.

For the first week or so, the puppies will "use up" more food than they eat. They will wade through it, sit in it, stamp it down and even actually eat some of it. With a fork, "fluff" up the food several times daily; that will keep their interest in it. Be sure to remove mother during feeding time or she will eat the pup's food. After the puppies have finished and you have taken out the pan, let mother in, and she will clean up the pen—and the pups—for you.

CARE FOR THE MOTHER

Two to three weeks after whelping, your mother will begin to look dragged out and quite thin, and her coat will be in poor condition. By starting to feed your pups at a young age (three to four weeks), you can relieve some of the stress on mother, particularly if she is caring for a large litter. Unless she already looks chunky, continue to feed her two meals or

even three meals a day until the pups are six or seven weeks old.

Once the pups start on solid food, mother will be ready for a "house cleaning." Give her a good grooming, trim her nails and brush out any dead coat. Brush out her skirts and clean her rear area well. Give her a bath. In other words, get her a new "dress." She will look, feel, and smell a lot better.

FOOD PANS

When feeding, use straight sided pans such as cake pans rather than pie pans. Less food will be pushed out of these pans. Finding pans low enough for the short-legged breeds can be a particular problem. Some frozen food trays work well, and they can go through the dishwasher. Styrene containers such as the kind used for meats in a butcher shop will also work very well.

WATER

Be sure your pups have water. For up to about six weeks they will not drink much, since there is a lot of water content in the gruel. However, they will drink some, and they should have a dish of water in the pen with them. You will have to teach them to drink. First, stir the water with your finger until the pups come up to the dish for a look. Then, gently push their noses into it. For a few days, they will "chew" the water, but once they become thirsty, they will start lapping. Remember to use a dish that is low enough for the dog to reach without tipping it over.

The epitome of the tolerant mother, this Brittany thinks it's high time for some serious weaning.

GENERAL INFORMATION

Mother will now spend four or five hours at a time out of the box. She will spend the night with the pups, and she will be eager to get into the box to clean it up after they have eaten. During this period, do not leave the food and water pans with the pups when mother is in the box. She will eat all the food, and if she doesn't sit in the water dish, she will drink that dry too. By four and a half or five weeks, mother will spend only the nights with the pups. Then, soon, she won't spend any nursing time with them and will stay only for very short play periods.

Because mother is nursing infrequently, milk production should start to decrease. Usually the breasts will dry up by themselves, and there will be no problem. This will happen gradually over a period of two weeks or so. Let the mother nurse when she feels like it, which will probably be once or twice a day for a few minutes. After a week you will notice that she plays with the pups but runs off when they start to nurse. You will hear a lot of "lip smacking" by the pups. This means that the milk is drying up. Pups will nurse up to eight weeks if the mother lets them, but usu-

BREEDERS' SURVEY

At what age do you start to wean your pups?

2 $\frac{1}{2}$ to 3 weeks <u>10</u>

3 $\frac{1}{2}$ to 4 weeks <u>4</u>

Over four weeks <u>10</u>

Do you start on puppy chow? <u>14</u>   *Baby food?* <u>13</u>

Comment: "I used to always start puppies with baby cereal, baby meat, egg yolk and canned milk whether I started at three weeks, four weeks or older. I do not, of late, follow this program. I have gone straight to puppy chow, soaked and then put through the blender (if the pups are very young) or simply mashed with a fork. I used a lot of liquid to make it very mushy. I have never force-weaned a litter. I allow the mother to do it slowly, and I fill in where she starts to leave off. The dams dry up slowly and nicely without any trouble, and I have never had a female with a sagging stomach; quite the contrary, they have super tight stomachs."

ally too many pups teeth biting on the nipples causes discomfort—and causes a loss of interest.

DAILY PUPPY CARE

At about four or five weeks your puppies are eating and drinking well and are aware of each other and of their surroundings. Mother is spending less and less time with them, and she is probably not sleeping with them. Once the mother leaves the pen at night, keep the pan of food in the pen during the night so that the pups can eat whenever they are hungry. Also keep the water dish in the pen.

They will now be playing with each other and beginning to show an interest in toys. A cotton sock, tennis ball and paper tubes from toilet paper rolls or towel rolls all make good play toys. The pups still sleep about eighty percent of the time.

Now is the time to rearrange your whelping box, changing it from a whelping box to a puppy pen. If you have a large litter, you may want to remove the pups to an exercise pen. If you have a large litter of large pups, you may want to fence off an area of the basement for them. If you use a pen and have it sitting on a rug or carpet, put a heavy duty plastic runner (available at a discount store) over the rug and then put your newspapers over it. Put a towel at one end of the pen and

As your puppies grow, you can turn your whelping box into a safe puppy pen. Add toys and comfortable bedding to make the puppies feel at home.

some shredded newspapers at the other end. Shredded paper absorbs urine and feces, helping to keep the pups clean.

Unless you hand-raised the litter, your work is really beginning. Up to now mother has done all of the feeding and cleaning. You have watched, smiled and changed the box once a day. Now, you will do it all, except that everything will be bigger and wetter.

When your mother ceases to nurse, you have to clean the box or pen two or three times a day—usually at least every A.M. and P.M. I still like to use towels, and I leave the sweater in the pen. Put the sweater on the same end as the towel. Feed the pups on the paper end. Most pups will eat and exercise on the papers—and sleep on the towel or sweater. Change the towel once or twice a day. Occasionally you will have a slow litter. The pups will sleep on the newspapers and exercise on the

towels. If this group doesn't change its habits quickly, remove the towel since your washer will be over-worked. It's good to continue to use the towels if possible because they give the pups good footing.

Continue the daily checks of the pups' eyes, ears, nostrils, and rears. It is important to check the rear ends at this age, since the mother no longer cleans the pups. Make sure that the rears are trimmed and clean. For heavy-coated breeds, trim the hair on the fannies, since feces can collect around the rectum. If this area is not kept clean, feces can quickly block the anal opening, and, in short order, a messy problem will develop. If this should happen, gently try to pull away whatever feces you can and then take a damp cloth and soak off the remainder. With scissors, trim away any feces that is left and then trim the hair back.

When your pups get older, you will have to take over the responsibility of cleaning and grooming them and checking them carefully for any skin or health problems. These English Cocker toddlers look very well cared for. Breeder, Paul Hussa.

Puppies From Four to Eight Weeks

SOCIALIZING

The puppies are weaned and are beginning to become aware of a world larger than their whelping box. Now is the time to start socializing your pups. They should be starting out with easy-going dispositions that only need care and time to bring them to full bloom. One or two youngsters in the household can help tremendously with the socializing process. Mother will also help by playing with the pups and pushing them around. She may attempt to run away, though, when the pups try to nurse on her. The nursing instinct is strong and lasts a long time in puppies.

For about ten minutes in the morning and in the evening, sit on the floor with your pups and let them climb over and around you. Handle them and talk to them. Not only is this socialization good for them but it also gives you an opportunity to access each pup individually. Unless you are really busy, you will find yourself spending more than ten minutes each play period.

A good relationship with the dam is the stepping stone to the proper socialization of your puppies. This five-week-old Doberman pup is cleaning mom's face.

Once the pups have been properly vaccinated let them meet all kinds of people, including children. Socialization like this will better prepare them for living in their new homes. Shar-Pei pups owned by Alice Lawler.

Weather permitting, you can let your puppies exercise outside, but supervise them carefully and watch your step!

Do not let your pups run on a tile or wooden floor. It may be fun to watch them slide and slip, but you don't help the pups—or their motor reflexes. Get them on the kind of flooring that gives them good footing. By four or five weeks, provided the weather is good, they can run outside several times a day. Use the "puppy shuffle" when walking through or around them. Do not raise your feet off the ground more than an inch or so, or you may inadvertently kick one halfway across the room.

At about four weeks, the personality of each litter becomes apparent. Litters as a whole are either: clean, quiet, neat, noisy, dirty and/or mean. The best litter is the clean, quiet and neat one. They sleep all night on their sweaters, exercise on the papers and stand outside their pans to eat their food. The worst is the noisy, dirty and mean group. These pups rise at five A.M., screaming to be let out of their pen. They sleep in the newspapers, exercise on the sweater (or in their food or water pan); and, when fully mobile, this group nips your ankles, hangs onto each other's tails and, in general, acts "wild." You'll drink a toast to each of these rascals as he or she goes off to a new home! Terrier breeders love this kind of litter, as they have *spirit* and really *show* in the ring, provided the breeder survives long enough to get them into the ring.

SOME COMMON—AND NOT SO COMMON—PUPPY PROBLEMS

Worms

One of the more common puppy problems is worms. Worms should be taken care of as soon as possible, since a puppy full of worms is not a thrifty puppy. (A "thrifty" puppy is a healthy puppy. You could say that the Miss Americas look "thrifty.") When you take your pups in for shots at five or six weeks, take a stool sample along for analysis. If your pups are wormy, the veterinarian will give you the proper medication needed to clean them up.

Roundworms are the most common of worms and don't be surprised or alarmed if your puppies have them. If the puppy is fairly wormy, you may see roundworms in his stool—or he may vomit up one or two worms. An adult roundworm is three to six inches long and white in color. It will coil up shortly after it is expelled, and it does not live long once exposed to air.

Your veterinarian will check the stool sample that you bring in, and he will tell you if your pups have worms. He will give you a worming medication, and your pups should be cleared up of roundworms after one or two treatments. First and second time whelpers often find roundworms difficult to cope with. If you are a beginning breeder, just remember that worms are common and that puppies from the best of homes have them.

A *very* wormy puppy will have an unthrifty appearance. His coat

The litter's personality will become apparent at about four weeks. These rambunctious Golden Retriever pups are just beginning to "raise Cane." Breeder, Nona Kilgore Bauer.

will be dull, his stomach distended, his eyes runny and his manner listless. Early worming can clear up these conditions quickly. Roundworms are the only worms that you can see in the stool. If your pups are infected with hookworms and/or whipworms, your veterinarian will give you a medication that will take care of all the worms. Follow your veterinarian's instructions about how often to worm and when to bring stool samples in for analysis. You can start worming as soon as the pups are completely weaned. If you suspect worms, get a stool sample to the vet by four or five weeks for analysis.

PUPPY SHOTS

You should take your pups to the veterinarian at six to eight weeks for their first shots. Prior to this time, do not take them much beyond your yard and do not let strange dogs play with them. When the pups get their shots, be sure to get a form from your veterinarian stating which series he gave them and when the next shot is due. If you sell one of the pups, it is important to give the shot record to the new owner, who will pass it on to his veterinarian. One series of shots usually covers distemper, hepatitis, leptospirosis and parainfluenza.

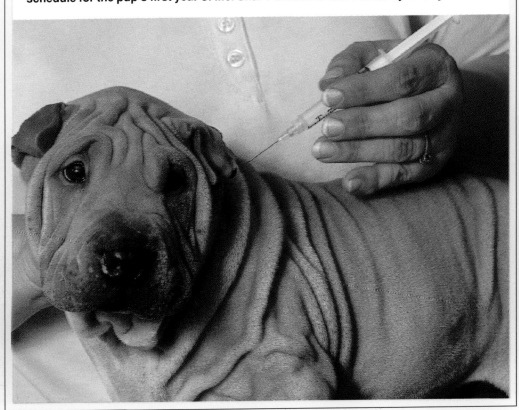

Your puppies should be taken for their first series of vaccinations at around six to eight weeks. The new owner's veterinarian will determine the most effective vaccination schedule for the pup's first year of life. Shar-Pei adolescent owned by Sherry Munsell.

PARVOVIRUS

In recent years, parvovirus has become a serious problem. Modified-live and killed vaccines are available, and you should discuss with your veterinarian whether or not to have these shots. The parvovirus shot can be given at the same time as the puppy shots.

Prevention is one of the best ways of combating parvo. When you have a young litter at home, do not allow strange dogs in your yard or in your house. When you return from a dog show, leave your shoes outside the door. Then, before handling your pups, change your clothes and wash up well. Simple precautions cannot hurt. Do not invite your dog-loving friends in after a show to look at pups. Have them come another day. It is so easy to bring things home from a dog show. It's certainly easier to bring home a bug than the Best in Show ribbon!

PUPPY BITES

Anytime after four weeks of age a lump may develop around a pup's neck, ears, penis or between the rear legs. This lump is almost always caused by a bite from another pup. When you examine the lump, you may find two puncture wounds, one on the front side of the lump and one on the back side. If the lump is large and in a touchy spot, you should probably see a veterinarian. Many of these wounds, however, can be cleared up with home remedies. Check the wound carefully and make sure that it is clean and not festering. Wash it off well, perhaps applying a little hot pack for a few minutes and then applying an antibiotic ointment several times a day. If a serious problem begins to develop after a day or so of home treatment or if festering continues, take the pup to the veterinarian. A shot of an antibiotic will usually produce a marked improvement within twenty-four hours. Puppies have quick recuperative and healing powers.

INJURIES

Again, prevention is the best guard against injuries.

1) Do not let your pups climb up on something and risk falling off.

2) Do not give them access to a swimming pool.

3) Do not give an eight-week-old pup access to the whole house.

Puppies like to wrestle and bite — they will each learn the limitations of play and rough-housing. "Hey, that hurts!"

4) Keep your pups penned in a small area when you are not home.

5) Do not leave an older dog with the pups when you are not home.

6) Teach young children how to handle puppies. Drops and falls can cause severe damage to a young pup.

Many injuries can be treated in the home. A limping puppy that has fallen off a step can be put in a separate pen for a few hours or a few days, depending on the nature and the severity of the injury. Surface wounds can be treated as above, and sometimes extra love and tenderness also produces miraculous recoveries. Puppies *scream*, often hysteri-cally, when they are hurt. Quiet them, hold them tightly and speak reassuringly to them. You will often find that the injury is not nearly as serious as the screams may have led you to believe.

Pups are very quick, and if you raise them for any length of time, you can expect to see a certain number of injuries. "Freak" accidents can happen—and they can happen quickly. You can eliminate some of them by following a few precautions. Remember, puppies that romp with large dogs in large, unsupervised areas can get hurt. Falls can cause serious injuries. Watch for electrical cords and extension cords; pups love to chew on these. Telephone cords

An outdoor exercise pen is handy for socializing the pups. These Great Pyrenees are basking in the morning sun.

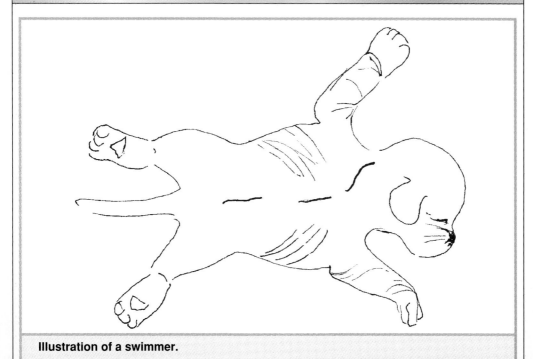

Illustration of a swimmer.

are also favorite objects on which to chew. Although these are not dangerous, the telephone company does get weary of having you on their doorstep every month looking for a new one.

On very rare occasions, an injury is so acute that you should consider putting a pup down. Always keep in mind not only the medical cost of repairing an injury but also the end result. Is it fair to sell a maimed pup to someone? *Can* you sell it? You are not doing anyone a favor by selling or given away a maimed or sickly pup. It may be difficult for you to put a pup down, but you will find it even more difficult coping with a dog's medical problem for years to come.

SWIMMERS

Swimmers are puppies that cannot stand on all four legs. This is not an uncommon problem, especially in heavy-bodied breeds. Make sure that your pups are standing, however unsteadily, around ten to fourteen days of age, and standing fairly steadily by three weeks—a good reason for providing secure footing for pups. If you see a pup on all fours—but wobbly—do not be concerned. This is not a swimmer but a puppy learning to walk.

Swimmers have a *turtle or pancake* look. The ribcage is abnormally large; they lie flat on their stomachs; and the rear legs— if not all four legs—stick out to either side. A swimmer must be brought up on his legs quickly. The longer he lies flat, the flatter the chest becomes. As the chest becomes flattened, the lung capacity decreases and death results.

The quickest way to get a swimmer up is to hobble him.

How to tape a swimmer.

The leg muscles on the pup are weak, and, therefore, his legs slip out to the side. The rear legs contain the muscles for pushing or propelling the dog. The front legs contain the muscles for pulling the dog. Your objective is to develop the inner thigh muscles of the rear legs. Therefore, you must hobble the dog on the *rear legs*. As the rear legs come up, the front legs will automatically come up. Once the dog is up on all fours, the problem will correct itself, and the dog will walk normally.

To hobble, wrap a piece of adhesive tape (about six inches long for a small to medium breed) around a rear hock, wrapping from the midpoint of the inside of the hock around to the outside and back around to the midpoint of the inside. Leave a "tab" on the tape facing toward the center. Perform the same procedure on the other leg, wrapping the tape from the inside of the hock around the back to the middle again. Connect the two tabs at about the width that you want the legs separated. Cut off the excess tape. Keep the hobble on for forty-eight hours. This will force the puppy to keep his legs under him when he walks.

After forty-eight hours or so, cut the tape *between* the legs and determine if he can stand on his own. If the pup is still wobbly, reconnect the center tape. (If you cut only the center tape, you will not have to tape around the hocks each time.) Pups usually get on their feet

with this treatment in three to four days. Some advise putting the puppy in a trough and pushing him up and down in it many times a day. However, the taping method is much quicker, and it is a surer way of getting a pup up on his legs.

Remember: A swimmer looks flat and turtle-like. Do not let a swimmer go for more than a few days before starting to work on him.

PROLAPSED RECTUM

Prolapsed rectum is not a common problem, but it can occur in a puppy that strains hard to have a bowel movement. The strain causes the lining of the anal canal to be pushed out, and this problem must be corrected immediately. Make a cold pack with a wash cloth. Hold the puppy upside down and push the tissue completely back in with the cold pack. Apply a little petroleum jelly to the anus and make sure that all hair is trimmed around it. Watch the stools to see if the pup has diarrhea or is constipated.

Puppies need plenty of exercise and play to keep healthy and strong. These two Chance R' Goldens are playing with a hunting bumper. Breeder, Nona Kilgore Bauer.

(Diarrhea is more common than constipation.) Contact your veterinarian for the proper treatment if the pup has either of these problems.

Keep an eye on a prolapsed rectum. If the prolapse reoccurs, push the rectum back in again. If the problem appears to be a chronic one, take the pup to the veterinarian. He will take a stitch in the rectum to repair it. (Yes, my pup said it *hurt*.) Do not let any protruding tissue dry out, since this will cause further complications.

UMBILICAL HERNIAS

Umbilical hernias are more common in some breeds than in others. They are caused by a delayed closure of the umbilical ring, and the hernia looks like a "lump" in the area where the umbilical cord was attached. An umbilical hernia rarely causes a problem, and small ones need not be repaired. If you have a pup with the problem, have it checked out by the veterinarian on a routine visit for shots.

COCCIDIOSIS

Coccidiosis is a protozoan disease that can affect young pups after they are six weeks of age. The signs of coccidia are a very loose stool—or bloody diarrhea—and a very unpleasant and strong smell in the stool. Coccidiosis can be transmitted from the mother if she is a carrier, or it can be picked up from a crate, carpet or kennel. It is a self-limiting disease, but while it's running its course it can run a pup down. If you suspect coccidiosis, have a stool analysis done immediately and see your veterinarian for treatment. If your pups have coccidiosis, the complete litter will be infected.

"GLUTTONY SYNDROME"

Pups with the "gluttony syndrome" are overzealous and sloppy eaters. You may notice this behavior about a week after your pups start on solid food. Shortly after eating, one or more pups may suddenly start gagging, choking and running around in circles. The pup will gasp for breath, and his tongue may turn bluish in color. Within a few minutes he will resume normal breathing. At that point, you may feel that the crises is past and that he will survive. Later, when you pick him up, you will notice a disagreeable discharge coming from the nose—and a lot of "snorkling" sounds. Wipe of the discharge and put the pup back in the box. This pup is an over-enthusiastic eater. He dives head first into the food pan and shovels his way across, blowing bubbles all the way. When finished, he does the same thing in his water dish. Part of his food has gone up this nasal passage, thus all of the gasping, "snorkling" and discharge. Keep his nostrils clean, and within a week he will start eating properly—and the problems will stop. Most pups have sense enough to eat with a little more grace!

Love and affection are most important to prepare your puppy for his new home.

Wrapping Up the Litter

REGISTRATION FORMS, CONTRACTS AND BREEDING RECORDS

The Stud Contract is the first form that you will probably be associated with. The owner of the stud dog will have you sign it at the time of the breeding. The form will state the name of your bitch, the name of the dog to which she was bred, the amount of the stud fee and when payable—nearly always at the time of breeding. Other conditions will also be noted: for example the right of the owner of the stud to get pick of a puppy and, if there are no puppies from the breeding, the right to a second service. Read the contract over carefully before signing it and be sure you understand it. Do not ask the owner of the stud to wait for the stud fee until you sell the pups. He is selling you a *service*, and the fee is due at the time the service (mating) is performed. You should also receive a copy of the stud dog's pedigree along with the stud contract and the dates that the mating took place. You may want to keep a record in a notebook of all this information. Work up a copy of the pedigree of the prospective puppies and put this in the notebook. The next page in your notebook can contain your whelping record for this litter.

After the puppies are born, notify the owner of the stud dog and give him the following infor-

mation: date of the whelping, number of pups whelped, number of surviving puppies, possible cause of death of dead puppies, number of males and females and their colors. The owner of the stud dog will then send you a *Litter Registration Application* form put out by the American Kennel Club. He will complete Section A of the form, and you will complete Section B and send it, together with the registration fee, to the American Kennel Club. You may want to record in your book the date that you sent this application to the AKC. In about four weeks, the AKC will send you the *Dog Registration Applications*—also called the "blue slips." You will receive one blue slip for each puppy in the litter. This slip will show the AKC *litter registration number*. Record this number in your notebook.

You can register the complete litter yourself. A fee is required for each puppy that you register. If you do not want to register each puppy in the litter yourself, give one blue slip to the new puppy owner, and he will register his own puppy. If you do this, it is up to you whether to name the pup or to let the new owner name him. When submitting the blue slip to the AKC, be sure to provide the name of the dog (first and second choice—and no more than twenty-six letters) and the sex, and circle the color of the pup. You must

REGISTRATION FEE: $8.00
REGISTRATION AND PEDIGREE: $25.00
EACH SUPPLEMENTAL TRANSFER: $4.00

MAIL APPLICATION WITH FEE TO:
AMERICAN KENNEL CLUB, Inc.
5580 CENTERVIEW DR STE 200
RALEIGH, NC 27606-3390

The person who owns the dog at the time this application is submitted to the AKC has the right to name it. Names are subject to AKC approval and may not include numbers or punctuation, except a dash or apostrophe. AKC may assign a Roman numeral suffix

AKC DOG REGISTRATION APPLICATION

MUST BE SUBMITTED TO REGISTER DOG: ELIGIBILITY IS RESTRICTED IF RECEIVED AFTER **MAY 11 1996**

DOG'S
NAME
PRINT a unique name, one letter per box. Skip a box between words.

LITTER NUMBER **SN242724/05**

BREED **COCKER SPANIEL**
DATE OF BIRTH **JAN 9 1995**

SIRE   Ch Pretty Tough Guy
       SM XXXXXX/03   (1-93) OFA XXX

DAM   Ch Pretty Cute Kid
       SNO XXXXX/01   (7-94)

BREEDER   Jane Doe

LITTER   Jane Doe & Helen Smith
OWNER   300 Cocker Spaniel Street
          Anyplace, USA

CHECK HERE ☐ FOR REGISTRATION & PEDIGREE. EACH ITEM MAILED SEPARATELY. $25.00 FEE DOES NOT INCLUDE TRANSFERS.

© 1993, 1994 The American Kennel Club, Inc.

The AKC reserves the right to correct or revoke for cause any registration certificate issued. Any misrepresentation on this application is cause for cancellation and may result in loss of all AKC privileges for those individuals who violate the integrity of this application.

• IF NOT USED INDICATE SEX ABOVE AND RETURN TO AKC WITH EXPLANATION •
SEE REVERSE SIDE FOR BALANCE OF APPLICATION

CB

Litter owner must indicate sex & color

Circle the dog's sex **MALE   FEMALE**
Circle the **one color** and, if appropriate **one marking/pattern** that best describes the dog
OR write in a color description on the line at the bottom.

COLOR

007 BLACK
018 BLACK & TAN
176 SILVER
068 BUFF
140 RED
061 BROWN
262 BROWN & TAN
019 BLACK & WHITE
146 RED & WHITE
299 BUFF & WHITE
063 BROWN & WHITE
034 BLACK WHITE & TAN
066 BROWN WHITE & TAN

MARKING/PATTERN
036 ROAN

I hereby give permission to use my AKC registered Kennel Name _____ in naming _____ this dog

SIGNATURE OF OWNER OF KENNEL NAME

After your litter is born, you must notify the owner of the stud dog and register the litter with the American Kennel Club.

complete Section A on the reverse side. The new puppy owner completes Section B. In about four weeks, you will receive the AKC registration form for the individual dog(s). (If you have been slow in submitting the forms, and your puppy is now six months old, you may enter him in up to three shows using the litter registration number.)

The *Registration Certificate* can be kept in your notebook together with the other litter information. You will use this form when entering a dog show, since it contains the information you need on your entry form. If you sell a dog, complete the information under Section A on the back of the form and give the form to the new owner. He will complete the information in Section B and submit the form with the fee to the AKC. He will then receive a new Registration Certificate in his name. The name of the dog will remain the same regardless of how many times the dog is sold. The registration number and the

STUD SERVICE RECORD

No._____
Name of
Bitch _____

Reg. No. _____
Sire _____
Dam _____
Owner_____
Address _____
Tel. No _____
Bred to: _____
Reg. No. _____
Breeding Date:_____
Due Whelp Date: _____
Remarks:_____

STUD SERVICE CERTIFICATE

THIS IS TO CERTIFY THAT   No._____

Name of Bitch_____

Breed_____ Reg. No._____

Stud bred to _____

Reg. No._____Date of Service _____

At _____
                                        Address
_____Owner of Stud _____
        Date due to Whelp
Fee_____Address _____

name of the breeder will also remain the same for the dog's entire life. Only the name of the *owner* will change. If you sell the dog "without papers," you will retain the registration paper, and the dog will officially remain in your name.

sheet and file it in your notebook. The address for the American Kennel Club is 51 Madison Avenue, New York, NY 10010.

SELLING YOUR PUPS

The easiest puppy sale is an out-right sale: you get the price of

The easiest way to sell your pups is an out-right sale: you get your money, the buyer gets his puppy and you are assured the pup is going to a good home.

The American Kennel Club puts out an inexpensive, spiral-bound book called *Dog Ownership and Breeding Records.* The first half of the book is for recording ownership of a dog and a breeding record of that dog; the second is for recording the history of a litter produced by an individual dog. This is a useful book, but it is not really necessary if you have one or two litters. The AKC will send you one record sheet when you register your litter, and you can keep your information on that record

the puppy, and the buyer gets the puppy and the registration form. Complications arise when "strings" are attached to the puppy: for example, you get a pick puppy from a future litter, you get to pick the future stud dog, the new owner pays half the showing fees, etc. Unfortunately, many of these complicated contracts are made between friends, and misunderstandings can often develop. Be wary of puppies with "strings," and be sure that all parties fully

LITTER REGISTRATION APPLICATION

FEE: $18.00
Effective July 1, 1991, litter applications must be received within six (6) months of the date of whelping. Fee subject to change without notice. Do not send cash.

DO NOT WRITE IN SPACE ABOVE

To register a litter born in the U.S.A. out of an AKC registered female and sired by an AKC registered male of the same breed. Mail with fee to:

THE AMERICAN KENNEL CLUB, 5580 CENTERVIEW DRIVE SUITE 200, RALEIGH, NC 27606-3390

PLEASE READ REVERSE SIDE BEFORE COMPLETING APPLICATION

PRINT IN CAPITAL LETTERS ONLY – USE INK
ONLY THIS ORIGINAL FORM WILL BE ACCEPTED

BREED | **PLACE OF BIRTH OF LITTER: CITY** | **STATE**

Indicate number of living dogs in this litter on the date this application is submitted to AKC:

| MALES | FEMALES | Date of birth of Litter: (Use Numbers) | MONTH | DAY | YEAR |

AKC Champion Title (if any) — REGISTERED NAME OF SIRE — Other AKC Titles (if any) — AKC NUMBER OF SIRE

AKC Champion Title (if any) — REGISTERED NAME OF DAM — Other AKC Titles (if any) — AKC NUMBER OF DAM

SEC. A. OWNER OF SIRE ON DATE OF MATING COMPLETES THIS SECTION.

Name of Owner of SIRE — FIRST NAME & INITIAL — LAST NAME

I CERTIFY that the above-named Dam was mated to the above-named Sire and that the Sire was owned or co-owned by me on the date of mating.

Place of mating (check one): ☐ U.S.A. ☐ FOREIGN (Print country _____).

SIGNATURE of Owner or Co-Owner of Sire — Date of Mating: MONTH DAY YEAR

SEC. B. OWNER (OR IF LEASED, LESSEE) OF DAM ON DATE OF BIRTH OF LITTER COMPLETES THIS SECTION.
Note: If ownership of Dam changed while Dam was in whelp, *SEC. C* below must also be completed.

Name & Address of Owner (or if Leased, Lessee) of DAM — FIRST NAME & INITIAL — LAST NAME — STREET ADDRESS — CITY — STATE — ZIP

Please check one box.
☐ I witnessed the mating
☐ I did not witness the mating

Co-Owner (If any) of DAM — FIRST NAME & INITIAL — LAST NAME

Please check one box
THIS LITTER IS A RESULT OF:
☐ a natural breeding
☐ artificial insemination
SEE REVERSE SIDE FOR INSTRUCTIONS

I apply to register this litter and **CERTIFY** that I was the Owner, Co-owner, or Lessee of the above-named Dam on the date of birth of the Litter, and that this Dam was not mated to any other dog during her season. I further **CERTIFY** that all of the representations on this application are true. I agree to comply with AKC rules and regulations. I have read the "Notice" and instructions on the reverse side of the application.

SIGNATURE of Owner, Co-Owner or Lessee of Dam

SEC. C. DO NOT COMPLETE UNLESS OWNERSHIP OF DAM CHANGED OR LEASE TERMINATED WHILE DAM WAS IN WHELP.
Note: Before completing, carefully read instructions on reverse side.

Owner (or if Leased, Lessee) of DAM on Date of Mating — FIRST NAME & INITIAL — LAST NAME

Co-Owner of the DAM on Date of Mating — FIRST NAME & INITIAL — LAST NAME

Please check one box
☐ I witnessed the mating
☐ I did not witness the mating

I CERTIFY that I was the Owner, Co-owner, or Lessee of the above-named Dam on the date the Dam was mated to the above-named Sire. I CERTIFY that the Dam, while in my possession, was not mated to any other dog during her season.

SIGNATURE of Owner, Co-Owner or Lessee of Dam

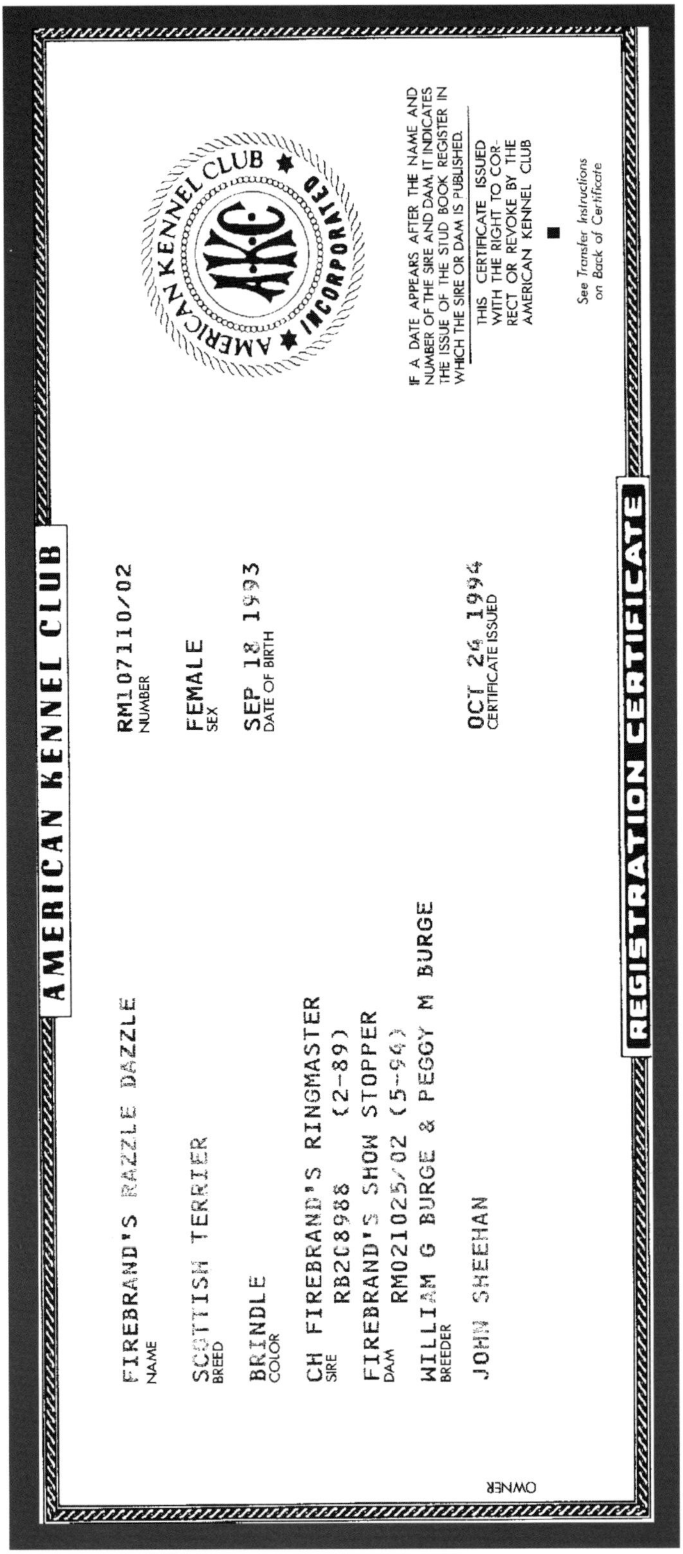

AMERICAN KENNEL CLUB

FIREBRAND'S RAZZLE DAZZLE
NAME

SCOTTISH TERRIER
BREED

BRINDLE
COLOR

CH FIREBRAND'S RINGMASTER
SIRE RB208988 (2-89)

FIREBRAND'S SHOW STOPPER
DAM RM021025/02 (5-94)

WILLIAM G BURGE & PEGGY M BURGE
BREEDER

JOHN SHEEHAN
OWNER

RM107110/02
NUMBER

FEMALE
SEX

SEP 18 1993
DATE OF BIRTH

OCT 26 1994
CERTIFICATE ISSUED

AMERICAN KENNEL CLUB INCORPORATED AKC

IF A DATE APPEARS AFTER THE NAME AND NUMBER OF THE SIRE AND DAM, IT INDICATES THE ISSUE OF THE STUD BOOK REGISTER IN WHICH THE SIRE OR DAM IS PUBLISHED.

THIS CERTIFICATE ISSUED WITH THE RIGHT TO CORRECT OR REVOKE BY THE AMERICAN KENNEL CLUB

See Transfer Instructions on Back of Certificate

REGISTRATION CERTIFICATE

understand all contracts. It is better to sell a puppy without strings than to lose a good friend at a later date. As they say, a good friendship will outlive a dog any day.

How or when you sell your puppies is up to you. Breeders surveyed tend to sell pet pups between eight to twelve weeks of age, with ten weeks being the average age. Those pups that are considered to have show potential are usually kept longer.

When a prospective buyer comes to look, show him the dam and *only* one or two pups that you have for sale. Do not display all of the pups and do not let him see the pups that you plan to keep. The more pups he sees, the more confused he will become. If you show him the one you plan to keep, he will know that this pup is the most desirable and that will be the one he wants—he won't want second best.

The puppy should look his "Sunday best," with nails trimmed and coat cleaned and groomed. Show the puppy in an area that he is familiar with, rather than showing him in a room that he has never seen before. If you sell

A perspective buyer should be shown only the dam and a few puppies you plan to sell. This is Ch. Misty Moor's Wee Nessie and her Cairn Terrier pups owned by Dawn Burdick.

one of your pups, provide instructions on feeding and also provide a record of the shots that he has had. Give the new owner one or more lessons on the proper grooming of the breed. If it is a heavily groomed breed (such as a Poodle), recommend a grooming shop that can groom and clip the breed to look somewhat like the standard. Give the new owner the instructions for registering the dog with the AKC together with the Registration Certificate (blue slip).

When the pup goes to his new home, cut the apron strings. Assume that you have done your best and be assured that the pup is going into a good home. Homes that have had a dog for eight, ten or twelve years always speak well for themselves. A dog that lives to ten years has received good care. A puppy buyer whose last two dogs were hit by cars does not carry a very high reference. Tell the new owner to call you if he has any problems. You will hear from some every week for a while, while others will never call again. Don't call them; they will tell you about problems that they normally

would not bother you with. When you sell the dog, give the registration papers to the new owners together with the responsibility of caring for the pup.

Encourage the new dog owners to buy a crate to keep the dog in when they are not at home. It is much easier to train a pup when there is a crate. You may want to suggest a good book about the breed. There are books for many breeds, and they range from inexpensive paperbacks to expensive hardcovers. Even those who buy a dog only for a pet often like to know a little about the breed. It is a nice gesture to give the new owner an inexpensive paperback book about the breed at the time he picks up the puppy. You should also give the new owner the name of the dog food that you have been feeding and the amounts that should be fed. Some breeders send along a little "care package" that includes the registration papers, the pedigree, the record of shots, a small bag of puppy chow, a leash, and a breed book or a pamphlet on puppy care. This care package gives the new owner a few days to get his needed supplies together.

Send your puppy out into the world with the confidence that you have done your best and the willingness and knowledge to answer any questions new owners may have.

Some Conclusions

You are now through your whelping and puppy rearing: your questions have been answered and your problems solved. Keep a few things in mind:

1) Puppies take time, and they are a lot of work.

2) Puppies will cost you more money than you may recoup through puppy sales. Do not expect to make money on your litter.

3) Do not have a litter unless you can keep one or two puppies until they reach the age of six months or so. You cannot count on selling all of your puppies at the age of two or three months.

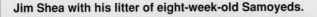
Jim Shea with his litter of eight-week-old Samoyeds.

4) If you are going to have a litter, take the time and effort to produce and raise the healthiest and happiest pups that you can.

Chances are good that you will not have any of the problems mentioned in this book. I have written about things that *can* happen, not about problems that *will* happen. I have tried to help you become aware of the problems, to recognize them, and then to take the appropriate action. Talk to other breeders in your breed, read up on your breed, and acquire some knowledge about breeding, whelping and puppy problems. All whelpings are different. If you are raising Pomeranians, you will have more problems than you would with a Coonhound that produced twelve pups—all of which lived—in a box in the garage. If you are raising a litter of Westies, you will have more problems than the breeder of Old English Sheepdogs. And if you raise a litter of Bulldogs, you will probably have more problems than anyone else!

Beginner's luck seems to hold true in whelpings. Many new breeders find that their first and second litters are a breeze and wonder what the whelping-problem talk is all about. The more litters you have, the more problems you will run into with both whelping and puppy rearing. You can breed for thirty years and still come upon something new. Use your common sense. Do not run to the veterinarian every day but have a good one available. If you do not let the litter dominate your life, you will find it a great experience. With a healthy attitude, you will cheer each little pup that goes off to his new home. When the last one leaves you may shed a tear and say "never again," but within a week you will be eyeing the pedigrees and working on your breeding program.

Good Luck! May you have an easy whelping, healthy pups and a Best in Show winner in your puppy box!

Clarisse, Maddy and Belle, two-week-old Tibetan Terriers, are perfect examples of darling, healthy, purebred puppies.

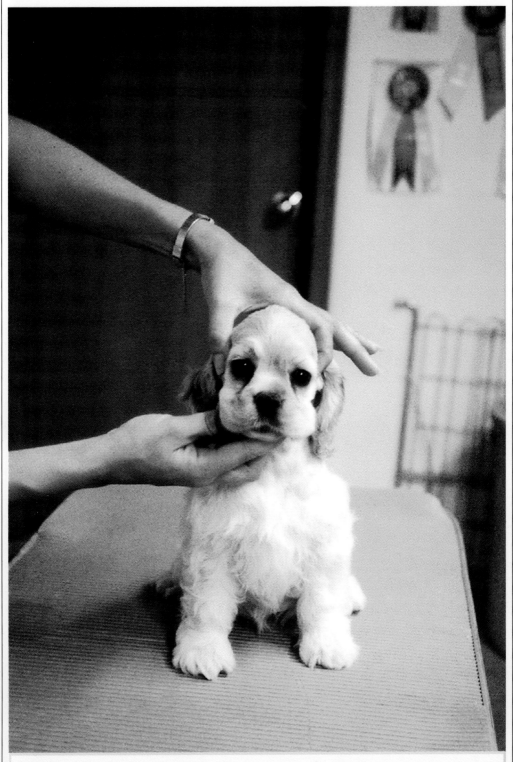

With some luck and perseverence, you may produce a possible future Best in Show winner!

INDEX

Absorption of whelps, 21
Afterbirth, 24, 26, 28, 29, 48
American Kennel Club, 112,
   114, 116
Antibiotics, 9
Artery forceps, 15, 29
Artificial respiration, 60

Bladder, 24, 23,
Boston Terrier, 37
Bottle feeding, 84
Brachycephalic breeds, 37
Breech presentation, 42
Breeding date, 8
Buffer rail, 31
Bulldog, 37, 45

Caked breasts, 77
Cannibalism, 64
Cesarean section, 37, 45—58
   —veterinarian, 47
   —deciding factors, 45, 46
Cleft palates, 31, 65
Coccidiosis, 110
Colostrum, 67
Constipation, 110
Contractions, 39, 41, 45

Defective pups, 65
Dehydration, 31, 72
—signs of, 72
Dewclaws, 68
Diarrhea, 110
Digital examination, 41
Discharge, 21

Distemper, 104
*Dog Ownership and Breeding
   Records*, 116
Dog Registration Application,
   112, 113

Eclampsia, 77, 78, 82
Edema, 65
Emergency veterinary service,
   46
Exercise, 32
   —during pregnancy, 9

Fading puppy syndrome, 72
Feeding
   —bottle feeding, 84
   —dog food, 9
   —formula, 84
   —hand feeding, 84
   —orphan puppy, 84—89
   —during pregnancy, 9
   —puppy, 36, 95
   —supplements, 9
   —tube feeding, 86—89
   —weaning, 94, 95
Food, 9
Food pans, 96
Formula, 84
Foster mothers, 83

Galactostasis, 77
Gavage method, 86
Gestation period, 9
Gluttony syndrome, 110
Grooming, 20

Hand-feeding chart, 87
Hand-raising puppies, 84
—bottle feeding, 84
—factors, 84
—tips, 92, 93
—tube feeding, 86, 87
Hare lip, 65
Healthy pups, 70
Hepatitis, 104
Hernia, 26
Hot water bottle, 14, 28, 32

Labor, 21, 22, 28, 38
—prolonged, 38
—temperature of mother, 23
Leptospirosis, 104
Litter Registration Application,
112, 117
Litter registration number, 112

Malpresentation, 38, 42, 43
Mammary glands, 20
Mastitis, 77, 78, 82
Mothers
—care, 67
—failure to accept pups, 79
—nursing, 55
Mummified puppy, 21, 66
Muzzle, 41

Nursing, 55
—problems, 77—82

Oil of camphor, 82
Orphan puppies, 82
—cleaning, 91
—feeding, 84—89
Ovary, 23, 24
Oxytocin, 29, 45

Palpation, 8
Parainfluenza, 104
Parvovirus, 105
Perpetual Whelping Calendar,
17, 19
Personality, 102
Placenta, 29
Pregnancy, 8, 9
—antibiotics, 9
—care, 9
—exercise, 9
—feeding, 9
—supplements, 9
—worming, 9
Presentation of whelp, 42
—breech, 42
—malpresentation, 38,42,43
—normal, 42
Prolapsed rectum, 109
Puppy
—bites, 105
—cleaning, 55
—daily care, 67, 98
—defective, 65
—dehydration, 72
—feeding, 36
—growth, 94
—healthy, 70
—injuries, 105
—newborn, 58
—personality, 102
—problems, 103—112
—selling, 116
—sickly, 70
—socialization, 100
—supplements, 36
—temperature, 34—36, 71
—weaning, 94
—weight gain, 70

Quartz heater, 32, 34

Ready box, 14
Reflector shade, 15
Registration Certificate, 114, 118
Respiratory problems, 72
Ringer's solution, 75
Roundworms, 103

Sac, 24, 25, 39
Selling the puppies, 116
Shaking down a puppy, 32, 56
Sickly pups, 70
—causes, 72
—death, 75
—feeding, 74
—handling, 73, 74
Slow starting pups, 58
—artificial respiration, 60
—resuscitation techniques, 58—61
—swinging, 59
Socialization, 100
Stud contract, 112
Stud service certificate, 115
Stud service record, 115
Super Moms, 62, 63
—supplements, 9, 36
Swimmers, 107—109
—hobbling, 107
—taping, 108, 109

The Gaines Progress Report, 67
Toxic milk, 72, 77, 78, 82
Tube feeding, 86—89
—advantages, 89

Umbilical cord, 26, 48, 62, 68
Umbilical hernia, 110
Uterine inertia, 38, 43, 55
Uterus, 23, 24, 48

Vaccinations, 104
Vagina, 23, 24, 39
Veterinarian, 14
—Cesarean section, 47
—emergency service, 46
—labor, 39, 41
—puppy care, 36
—traveling to, 47
—vaccinations, 104
Vulva, 20, 21, 40, 42

Water, 96
Waterbag, 23, 39
Weaning, 94—97
—mother care, 96
Whelping
—assisting, 25—31
—concerns, 21
—equipment, 13
—problems, 37
—temperature of mother, 17
Whelping box, 9, 10, 11, 14, 23, 53
—cleaning, 67
—environment, 31
—temperature, 31
Whelping chart, 44
Whelps, 8, 23
—absorption of, 21
—extra large, 39
Worms, 103

X-ray, 17

Suggested Reading

Owner's Guide to Dog Health
by Dr. Lowell Ackerman, DVM
TS-214

432 pages, over 300 color photographs

Winner of the 1995 Dog Writers Association of America's Best Health Book, this comprehensive title gives accurate, up-to-date information on all the major disorders and conditions found in dogs. Completely illustrated to help owners visualize signs of illness, different states of infection, procedures and treatment, it covers nutrition, skin disorders of the major body systems (reproductive, digestive, respiratory), eye problems, vaccines and vaccinations, dental health and more.

Dog Behavior and Training
by Dr. Lowell Ackerman, DVM
TS-252

292 pages, over 200 color photographs

Joined by co-editors Gary Landsberg, DVM and Wayne Hunthausen, DVM, Dr. Ackerman and about 20 experts in behavioral studies and training set forth a practical guide to the common problems owners experience with their dogs. Because behavioral disorders are the number-one reason for owners to abandon a dog, it is essential for owners to understand how the dog thinks and how to correct him if he misbehaves. The book covers socialization, selection, rewards and punishment, puppy-problem prevention, excitable and disobedient behaviors, sexual behaviors, aggression, children, stress and more.

Skin and Coat Care for Your Dog
by Dr. Lowell Ackerman, DVM
TS-249

224 pages, over 200 color photographs

Dr. Ackerman, a specialist in the field of dermatology and a Diplomate of the American College of Veterinary Dermatology, joins 14 of the world's most respected dermatologists and other experts to produce an extremely helpful manual on the dog's skin. Coat and skin problems are extremely common in the dog, and owners need to better understand the conditions that affect their dog's coats. This book details everything from the basic parasites and mange to grooming techniques, medications, hair loss and more.

Choosing a Dog for Life
by Andrew DePrisco
TS-257

Every owner's first choice for a selection handbook, illustrated with over 700 full-color photographs, this authoritative volume discusses the standards, health, growth, special needs, temperament and training of the most popular 166 dog breeds. Representing the first-hand experience and advice of hundreds of dedicated breeders and owners, this definitive and beautiful book is absolutely essential for anyone looking for a purebred dog.

A Canine Lexicon
by Andrew DePrisco and James Johnson
TS-175

An up-to-date encyclopedia dictionary for the dog person, this is the most complete single volume on the dog ever published. It covers more breeds than any other book as well as other relevant topics, including health, showing, training, breeding, anatomy, veterinary terminology, and much more. No dog book before has ever offered this many stunning color photographs of all breeds, dog sports and topics (over 1300 in full color).

The Atlas of Dog Breeds of the World
By Bonnie Wilcox, DVM and Chris Walkowicz
H-1091

This atlas traces the history and highlights the characteristics, appearance and function of every recognized dog breed in the world. 409 different breeds receive full-color treatment and individual study. Hundreds of breeds in addition to those recognized by the American Kennel Club and the Kennel Club of Great Britain are included —- the dogs of the world complete! The ultimate reference work, it includes comprehensive coverage and intelligent and delightful discussions. The prefect gift book. Over 110 full-color photographs.

The Mini-Atlas of Dog Breeds
by Andrew DePrisco and James Johnson
H-1106

Contains over 400 breeds illustrated with over 700 full-color photographs. This compact yet comprehensive book has been praised and recommended by most national dog publications for its utility and reader-friendliness. The true field guide for dog lovers.